eat * sleep * shop

LONDON

STYLE GUIDE

saska graville

photography by
jessica reftel evans & martin reftel

MURDOCH BOOKS

For Dad, who loved to travel the world,
but was always happiest coming home to London.

SHOP

1 *Rococo Chocolates*
2 *Green and Stone*
3 *Few and Far*
4 *Sigmar*
5 *Designers Guild*
6 *The Shop at Bluebird*
❋ *British Red Cross*
❋ *Oxfam*

EAT & DRINK

7 *Victoria & Albert*
   Museum Café

EAT, DRINK & SHOP

8 *The Conran Shop*

SLEEP

9 *Number Sixteen*

● **Tube Station**

❋ **Designer Charity**

Special mention to two of London's best charity shops—both are well worth a look for a designer bargain. The British Red Cross shop, tucked down a King's Road side street is famed for its haul of big name vintage and new labels. Sign up to the mailing list for the annual designer evening, with special donations from the likes of Chanel and Dolce & Gabbana. 69–71 Old Church Street, SW3 5BS. Tel 08450 547 101.
www.redcross.org.uk
At the branch of Oxfam further down the King's Road, you might find a Chanel bag or a pair of Prada shoes. With its old parquet floors and funky display cabinets, the shop is more like a designer boutique than a charity outlet. It's definitely worth popping in. 123a Shawfield Street, King's Road, SW3 4PL. Tel 0207 351 7979. www.oxfam.org.uk

61

contents

✳ welcome to london style — 4

✳ my 24-hour wishlist — 7

✳ hampstead — 8

✳ islington — 18

✳ primrose hill — 34

✳ bermondsey — 50

✳ chelsea & south kensington — 62

✳ clerkenwell — 76

✳ columbia road — 94

✳ london fields — 116

✳ stoke newington & dalston — 136

✳ shoreditch — 148

✳ bethnal green — 168

✳ kensal rise — 180

✳ notting hill — 194

✳ marylebone — 208

✳ bloomsbury — 228

✳ king's cross — 244

✳ soho & noho — 260

✳ off the map — 278

welcome to london style

I'M A LONDONER, BORN AND BRED and I love
my hometown. It has a personality and style all its own—
from grand to edgy, modern to heritage and urban to shabby
chic. London is such a vast, sprawling, living, breathing entity
that it's impossible to give it a neat and convenient label.
And that's what makes me love it all the more.

But there is, I believe, AN ESSENCE TO LONDON
STYLE, and you find it in the small, off-the-radar places: the
one-off shops, street markets, corner pubs and local restaurants
that Londoners themselves go to. These places share a certain
eccentricity, quirkiness and independence of spirit. And that's
what this book is all about.

You don't need me to tell you about the 'trophy' sites—the palaces,
museums, parks and famous shops—but I will share with you the
places that you're not going to find in an average guide book. I'll
tell you where to rummage for vintage furniture on a Saturday
morning (no, not Portobello market, everyone knows about that
and it's priced for tourists), the tiny A-list florist you'll fall in love
with (the one Nigella Lawson swears by), the local pub beloved by
the country's fussiest food critic and the two-bedroom B&B that
gets booked months in advance.

In other words, I'LL GET YOU UNDER THE SKIN OF
THIS INTOXICATING CITY, introducing you to the lesser-
known addresses and some of the people behind them. I make
no claims for this book as a comprehensive guide to London—I'm
assuming a certain amount of prior knowledge on your part of the
classics like Selfridges and Liberty—but it will give you the chance
to scratch the surface just a little bit more.

'A tiny, always-packed café, it's flying the flag for Best of British'

11

3*

2008 Syrah,
2008 Mouvedre, Al Moul...
2008 Merlot, Domaine Baptiste Lo...
2008 Malbec, Finca Los Primos, ...
2010 Rioja, 'L2', Telmo Rodriguez,
2009 Shiraz, Lantana, New Sout...
2006 Pinotage, Porter Mill Station
2006 Hegarty Chamans, Les Cha...
2008 Cabernet Sauvignon, Koyle, ...
2009 Pinot Noir, Forrest Estate, M...
2008 Montepulciano d'Abruzzo, Villa M...
2010 Valpolicella, Allegrini, Venet...
2008 Bordeaux Superieur, Chatea...
2008 Zinfadel, De Loach, San...
2010 Fleurie, Domaine de la M...
2007 Crozes Hermitage Les Pier...
2008 Givery 1er Cru, Domaine Lau...
2006 Chateauneuf du Pape, Domai...
2006 Chateau Barde-Haute, St...

3*

4*

4*

PRAWNS, CHILLI, GARLIC

MACKEREL, ORANGE, BLACK OLIVES

WHITEBAITS, FRIED EGG, PIQUILLO PEP

GIROLLES, RED ONIONS, MANCHEGO

SQUID, RUNNER BEANS

RAZOR CLAMS, CHORIZO, MINT

CHICKEN LIVERS, FINO

IBERICO PORK FILLET

CLAMS, TOMATO, JAMÓN

PADRON PEPPERS

to pick up some fish. Then I go for coffee at Monmouth (www.monmouthcoffee.co.uk) in Borough Market followed by food shopping with friends. Sundays are very lazy days for me. I'll pop into José for a glass of fino before heading to Roka in Canary Wharf (www.rokarestaurant.com) for dim sum, my favourite thing to eat on Sunday.

What's in your secret shopping address book?

Maltby Street for bread, vegetables and cheese. I love O'Shea's in Chelsea (www. osheasbutchers.com) for meat and Selfridges (www.selfridges.com) does a wonderful selection of Maldonado hams. Iberica near Oxford Circus (www.ibericalondon.co.uk) is great for Spanish delicacies.

Where's the best place for a weekend supper?

Apart from my restaurants, Zucca (as above), Le Caprice (www.le-caprice.co.uk) or **Pizza East** (see page 159). Zucca, Le Caprice because it's just so classy and 'English', and Pizza East because it's so much fun. It's always lively and buzzing and the pizza flavours are wonderful.

Best place for a drink?

Lounge Bohemia in Shoreditch (loungebohemia.com). Just such a cool venue and the cocktails are delicious and really creative.

Your favourite breakfast spot?

The Wolseley (www.thewolseley.com) because it's a stunning place to sit and eat really traditional, English food. Wonderful teas, too.

Top three things that every visitor to London should do?

Go to the National Gallery (www. nationalgallery.org.uk), Tate Modern (www.tate.org.uk) and the Anchor & Hope (36 The Cut, SE1 8LP. Tel 0207 928 9898) for a proper pint and delicious food.

'Maltby Street is a hotbed of the coolest new food suppliers'

How would you define London style?
London is the best city in the world—chic, stylish and where it all happens.

Where do you go in London to be inspired?
I love standing on the Millennium Bridge. Look one way and you have St Paul's and the Tower of London—two of the most beautiful old buildings in London. Look the other way you have the Tate Modern and the London Eye. Awe-inspiring.

Your favourite local places?
Maltby Street (see page 50) is a hotbed of the coolest new food suppliers and restaurants. I also love eating at Zucca in Bermondsey Street (www.zuccalondon.com), because the food is wonderfully fresh and seasonal and every time I go I am surprised by the menu and flavours.

Describe your perfect out-and-about weekend?
On Saturday I wake early and head to Billingsgate (www.billingsgate-market.org.uk)

josé pizarro

No visit to Bermondsey is complete without dropping into the restaurants owned by Spanish chef, José Pizarro: the corner tapas bar José and the larger Pizarro. Lucky locals to have these buzzy places in their midst. The smaller José is constantly packed (you can't book at either restaurant), serving authentic tapas washed down with Spanish wines, all in a funky setting of exposed brickwork and marble counter tops. Find a stool if you can (stand up if you can't) and enjoy the buzz. Two hundred metres down the road at Pizarro, with its booths and private dining room, the roomier space means you'll get a seat, but be prepared to wait. Dishes are larger than the tapas served at José, but the mood is still one of sharing delicious food with friends and enjoying cava, wine and sherry from independent Spanish producers.

JOSÉ AND PIZARRO
✽ **José** ✽ **104 Bermondsey Street SE1 3UB**
✽ **Pizarro** ✽ **194 Bermondsey Street SE1 3TQ** ✽ *www.josepizarro.com* ✽ **0207 354 8181**

'When it comes to foodie credentials, Maltby Street is rapidly gaining first place'

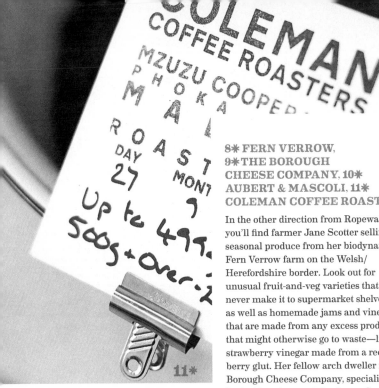

8✳ FERN VERROW, 9✳ THE BOROUGH CHEESE COMPANY, 10✳ AUBERT & MASCOLI, 11✳ COLEMAN COFFEE ROASTERS

In the other direction from Ropewalk you'll find farmer Jane Scotter selling seasonal produce from her biodynamic Fern Verrow farm on the Welsh/Herefordshire border. Look out for unusual fruit-and-veg varieties that never make it to supermarket shelves, as well as homemade jams and vinegars that are made from any excess produce that might otherwise go to waste—like strawberry vinegar made from a recent berry glut. Her fellow arch dweller is The Borough Cheese Company, specialising in the French mountain cheese Comté and delicious Comté biscuits made from any otherwise-wasted end pieces. They are also experimenting with making a Cheshire cheese on the arch premises. Organic wine importer Aubert & Mascoli and coffee suppliers Coleman Coffee Roasters complete this arch's roll call of traders.

55 Stanworth Street
SE1 3NY
www.fernverrow.com,
www.boroughcheesecompany.co.uk,
www.aubertandmascoli.com,
www.colemancoffee.com

12✳ TAYSHAW

A huge arch space is packed with an incredible variety of fruit and veg from this ex-Borough Market favourite. Expect to find queues for the likes of new-season girolles, heritage tomatoes and short-season white asparagus. One of the area's busiest businesses.

60 Druid Street
SE1 2EZ

Terschelling
Schapenkaas
Organic, pasteurised
sheeps milk gouda made with
vegetarian rennet.
Handmade on the £28.50
Island of Terschelling per kg

3✳ TOPOLSKI, 4✳KASESWISS, 5✳JACOB'S LADDER FARMS

Keep heading down Druid Street and you'll find the arch occupied by Polish produce importers Topolski. Don't leave without buying some of their hot smoked sausages (flavoured with the likes of marjoram, caraway and juniper), and a jar of beetroot with horseradish to serve on the side. In the same arch is KaseSwiss—specialising in traditional farmhouse cheeses from Switzerland, such as Gruyère, emmental and gouda with cumin—along with Jacob's Ladder Farms selling meat from a collective of Sussex farms. Get to the meat counter early and you'll also find bread baked by local bread maker Andy in his Brixton back garden. He only makes about ten loaves a week to sell here, using a 1950s flour mill in his kitchen and a wood-fired oven in his back garden, and they sell out fast.
Arch 104, Druid Street
SE1 2HQ
www.topolski.co.uk, www.kaseswiss.com, www.jacobsladderfarms.co.uk

6✳ THE HAM & CHEESE COMPANY, 7✳THE KERNEL BREWERY

Turn right off Druid Street and head underneath the railway line and you'll come to more producers on Ropewalk. At The Ham & Cheese Company, you'll find charcuterie and cheese sourced from small, independent suppliers in France and Italy and then matured underneath the railway arches. The damp brickwork and cool temperatures provide ideal conditions, apparently. And in the same arch is The Kernel Brewery, where brewer Evin O'Riordain creates and bottles his award-winning pale ales and stouts. Grab a bottle, a few slices of something tasty from The Ham & Cheese Company and sit at one of the trestle tables outside. Delicious.
1 Ropewalk
SE1 2HQ
www.thehamandcheeseco.co.uk, www.thekernelbrewery.com

London is, of course, huge and even Londoners are pretty clueless about its geography when you transplant them out of their comfort zones. IT'S IMPOSSIBLE TO COVER IT ALL IN ONE GO, so don't even try. Instead, tackle it an area at a time. I've divided the city geographically into North, South, East, West and Central, and then within each area are the 'villages' that create London's personality. My advice? Pick an area, go for a wander in one village, and then get yourself an Oyster travel card (for all London travel) to zip off to another one in the same area.

Within each village, I've included a mix of the most stylish and individual places for shopping, eating, drinking and sleeping—all the important things. I'll also introduce you to some of the Londoners themselves, who I've persuaded to share their favourite local haunts. From fashion to furniture to food, I'll direct you to the spots that you won't find on the average high street. I'll give you options for breakfast, lunch, supper and everything in between. And when it comes to a bed for the night, I'll point you in the direction of some of the city's sleekest check-ins (some tiny, some a little bit grander).

Enjoy your time in my hometown. I hope that this book reveals a side to my city that you wouldn't otherwise have seen. There'll always be somewhere new to discover and that's the joy that is London—one trip is never enough. See you again soon.

my 24-hour wishlist

Let's pretend that geography is no object. If I could plot my perfect London day from the places featured in this book, here's where I'd go:

I'd start with breakfast at **Granger & Co** (see page 288)—no one does scrambled eggs and a flat white as well as Bill Granger. I'd avoid the Portobello Market crowds, and go instead to nearby **Golborne Road** (see page 194), where the cluster of interiors shops sells some of the most interesting homewares in London. Then I'd head over to **Bermondsey** (see page 50) to do my food shopping from the producers who have decamped to Maltby Street and its surrounds from the (much busier) Borough Market. Lunch would be at **Pizza East** in Shoreditch (see page 159), followed by a stroll along **Columbia Road** (see page 94), buying flowers and popping into the quirky, independent shops that open only at the weekend. Shopping and eating done, I'd check in to **Dean Street Townhouse** in Soho (see page 272), for a night of urban luxury in one of my favourite hotels. A perfect day.

PS Were I a bit more adventurous, I'd book in to **The Family Business** (see page 90) for a work-of-art tattoo, but I'll leave that for someone else's dream day.

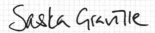

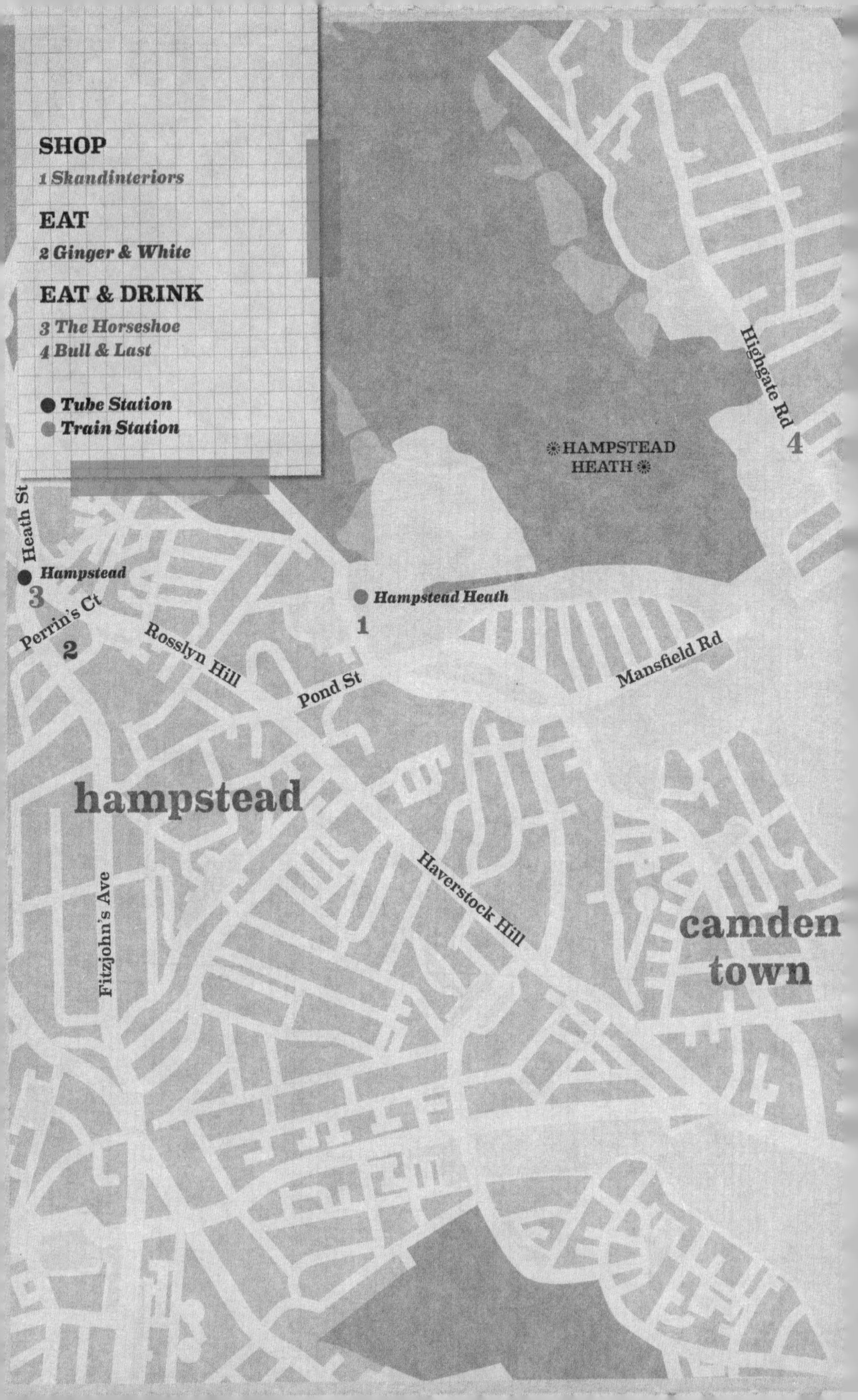

SHOP

1 *Skandinteriors*

EAT

2 *Ginger & White*

EAT & DRINK

3 *The Horseshoe*
4 *Bull & Last*

● *Tube Station*
● *Train Station*

Highgate Rd

4

❀HAMPSTEAD
HEATH ❀

Heath St

● *Hampstead*
3

● *Hampstead Heath*

1

Perrin's Ct

2

Rosslyn Hill

Pond St

Mansfield Rd

hampstead

Fitzjohn's Ave

Haverstock Hill

camden
town

N Hampstead

Undoubtedly one of London's most beautiful areas, with the 790 acres of wild and unspoilt Hampstead Heath on its doorstep and the sort of grand residential architecture that most of us can only dream of. Shopping-wise, it tends towards chain stores and slightly twee, overpriced interiors shops, with not as many cool, independent places as you might hope for. But it's worth a visit nonetheless. Get lost on the Heath and then head to one of the area's pubs for a long lunch.

north

2✳ GINGER & WHITE

Search out this small enclave of pared back urban chic amid the tweeness of the rest of Hampstead. A tiny, always-packed café, it not only serves some of the best coffee in London, but it's flying the flag for Best of British. Your sausage sarnie boasts Wicks Manor sausages, free range eggs are from Treflach Farm and the goat's cheese is Capricorn Somerset. Sit at the communal wooden table, gazing at the Union Jack print and jar of wild English flowers, and the effect is all very Cool Britannia.

4a–5a Perrin's Court
NW3 1QS
0207 431 9098
www.gingerandwhite.com

bermondsey

south

This part of London will never win prizes for prettiness, but when it comes to foodie credentials, it's rapidly gaining first place. The Victorian railway arches along Maltby Street, Rope Walk, Stanworth Street and Druid Street house a collective of passionate retailers that rival the nearby and more famous foodie mecca of Borough Market—many of the stallholders used to be Borough regulars but have decamped here to what has been christened Maltby Street Market. Most of the companies use the space as the weekday base for their wholesale businesses, only opening to the public on a Saturday morning (9 am–2 pm). Check ahead before you visit. There is talk of some producers moving to a new site nearby, but nothing confirmed. Either way, this is one of London's new must-visits for anyone who loves good food.

1✳ ST JOHN BAKERY COMPANY

Chef Fergus Henderson is one of London's favourite restaurateurs and this is the baking arm of his business (see page 81 for his flagship St John restaurant). During the week, the bread made here supplies Henderson's three restaurants as well as other food shops but on a Saturday morning it opens to the public. With baker Justin Piers Gellatly at the helm, things are kept simple—a concrete floor, corrugated iron roof and a table piled high with some of Britain's best bread. Sourdoughs, ryes and soda bread are quickly snapped up, but it is the company's custard doughnuts and mini Eccles cakes that really draw the crowds.
Arch 72, Druid Street
London SE1 2DU
www.stjohnbakerycompany.com

2✳ BEA'S OF BLOOMSBURY

Next door to St John Bakery, the railway arch space has been hung with floral bunting, some chairs and tables set up and a pretty cake shop atmosphere created. Once again, there are no fancy fittings, but the creations are so enticing that you'll want to take your pick and linger with a cup of coffee. How to choose from a pile of giant chocolate and strawberry meringues, Bea's famous 'duffins' (a blend of doughnut and muffin), cupcakes, and mouth-watering peanut butter and jam slices? Buy something to eat now—and something else to take away.
Arch 76, Druid Street
London SE1 2HQ
www.beasofbloomsbury.com

6*

THE KERNEL BREWERY LONDON

STELLA

5.1% ABV

THE KERNEL BREWERY LONDON

PALE ALE
BEER DE SAUVIN

5.3% ABV

THE KERNEL BREWERY LONDON

PALE ALE
BEER DE SAUVIN

5.3% ABV

THE

7

3*

CARNE SALATA — £50

SAUCISSE SECHE — £45

JESUS DU PAYS BASQUE — £

CHORIZO — £33.5

CHEESE

PARMIGIANO REGGIANO — £29

MOZZARELLA DI BUFALA
250g — £5.90
2 × 100g — £4.90
100g — £2.90

6

helen reece

You'll want everything in this sleek, chic interiors store. Skandinteriors has a carefully chosen selection of the best of Skandi style, with stock ranging from larger pieces like a Danish armchair or a mid-century sideboard to coffee pots, cushions and vases. Owner Helen Reece started her career as an actress, but after meeting legendary Biba founder Barbara Hulanicki, she became her assistant and a passion for design was born. Since then, she's worked as an interior designer and started several businesses, the latest of which is Skandinteriors. Helen does all the buying, and her taste is spot on. She's also careful not to overprice her wares, which is refreshing in a postcode where retailers habitually add a few 00s onto the end of the price.

SKANDINTERIORS
57 Southend Road NW3 2QB ❖ 07794 640 937 ❖

3✹ THE HORSESHOE

A gastro pub with X factor, not only is the food great and the room lovely, but the place brews its own ales. The main room boasts big wooden tables, giant windows and cool art on the walls. So far, so not your average pub. And how many pubs credit the provenance of the food on the menu—St Austell Bay mussels, roast Cornish cod and all the meat from one Suffolk butcher who uses local farms. The perfect spot for a long Sunday lunch, or just a quick drink at the bar.
28 Heath Street
NW3 6TE
0207 431 7206

4✹ BULL & LAST

No wonder one of the UK's most influential food critics, Giles Coren, loves this pub so much, raving about the 'best pub food' he's ever eaten. Technically in Highgate, but right on the edge of Hampstead Heath, it's everything a neighbourhood local should be: outstanding food, a great room to hang out in and some of the friendliest staff in London. Nothing to find fault with. There's even a canine menu for your four-legged friend, featuring pig's ears and roast marrow bones. Pop in for Sunday lunch and you'll find the likes of crisp pig's cheek, basil, watermelon, mint and sesame on the menu—a cut above the usual pub grub. And don't leave without trying the Scotch eggs sold at the bar—worth a visit for one of those alone. If the weather's nice, order a picnic hamper and head over the road to Hampstead Heath; how many pubs offer a service like that?
168 Highgate Road
NW5 1QS
0207 267 3641
www.thebullandlast.co.uk

'London breaks rules, it doesn't fit into any box'

How would you define London style?

It can be edgy and chic, playful and sophisticated. It borrows from every decade. If you go to different countries they have a real look, but London breaks rules, it doesn't fit into any box. London likes to make a statement.

Where do you go in London to be inspired?

The South Bank (www.southbankcentre. co.uk); I love the Thames with theatre, film, art and music right on its banks. It's a great place to sip a drink and watch the world go by. I also love Hampstead Heath (www. hampsteadheath.net). It's on my doorstep and never fails to inspire.

Describe your perfect out-and-about weekend?

I love a night at the theatre: the National is always a pleasure (www.nationaltheatre. org.uk), plus the Royal Court (www. royalcourttheatre.com) and the Donmar (www.donmarwarehouse.com).

15

Where's the best place for a weekend supper?

The Gavroche in Mayfair (www.le-gavroche.co.uk) is a real experience and special treat. But the best time to go is their weekday lunchtime deal— out of this world food, endless courses and beautiful wine included. It's easy to lose a whole afternoon.

Best place for a drink?

Some of my favourite spots are the homely locals in Hampstead; The Holly Bush (22, Holly Mount, NW3 6SG) and The Stag (www.thestaghampstead.com) are the perfect hideaways for a nightcap.

Your best breakfast spot?

The Wolseley in Piccadilly (www.thewolseley.com) can't be beaten.

Where do you go in London to relax?

The Berkeley hotel spa (www.the-berkeley.co.uk); it has a beautiful rooftop pool where you can sit in the sun and pretend you're on holiday.

Your local Hampstead tips?

Go to the best cinema ever, the Hampstead Everyman (www.everymancinema.com), then have a long walk on Hampstead Heath, finishing with a cake in Kenwood House (www.english-heritage.org.uk). Goldfinger's modernist house at 2 Willow Road (www.nationaltrust.org.uk) is also well worth a visit.

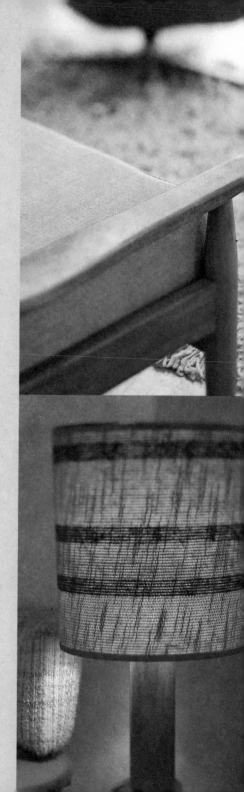

17

SHOP

1 *Fandango*
2 *Palette*
3 *Annie's*
4 *Labour of Love*
5 *Atelier Abigail Ahern*

EAT & DRINK

6 *The Drapers Arms*
7 *The Elk in the Woods*
8 *Ottolenghi*
9 *The Duke of Cambridge*

● Tube Station
● Train Station

● Highbury & Islington

Islington Park St

2 Cannonbury Ln

Cannonbury Rd

4

Upper St

Barnsbury St

8

Essex Road

6

Almeida St

Cross St

1

5

islington

Theberton St

Barnsbury Rd

Essex Rd

Packington

Liverpool Rd

St Peter's St

3 7

9

Charlton Pl

● Angel

Pentonville Rd

City Rd

N

islington

There's nothing up and coming about Islington; it is well and truly up and come. Upper Street offers an endless choice of smart shops and cafés, while picturesque Camden Passage is a treasure trove of vintage and antique boutiques and market stalls. In leafy Barnsbury, you'll find streets of elegant white houses—former British Prime Minister Tony Blair was a local—and chic gastro pubs. No wonder Islingtonites can't imagine living anywhere else.

north

1*

1*

2*

2*

1✷ FANDANGO

Billed as 'sustainable luxury', this tiny wedge-shaped store has a small but perfectly formed selection of wares, all of them with a glossy edge. From rare nineteenth-century sunburst mirrors to Murano glass apothecary jars and sets of antlers, everything has been beautifully restored. This is not the place for shabby chic. Instead, anything you pick will add a bit of drama and glamour to your home. A treasure trove.

2 Cross Street
N1 2BL
Tel 07979 650 805
www.fandango.uk.com

2✷ PALETTE

This is an unmissable shopping spot for anyone serious about vintage buys. Owner Marco Ellis is dedicated to sourcing the very best quality clothes and accessories. With an eagle eye for a design classic, his stock puts the best of the old alongside a well-chosen smattering of emerging contemporary labels. The mix is unique. Actress Emma Watson—no slouch in the fashion stakes—is a fan, wearing one of Palette's Ossie Clark dresses to a film premiere. It's the sort of shop to lose an afternoon in. Take advantage of Marco's pin-sharp fashion sense and come away with something that you'll wear forever. A shop move is planned in 2012, so check the website before visiting.

21 Canonbury Lane
N1 2AS
Tel 0207 288 7428
www.palette-london.com

3✳ ANNIE'S

When you can boast Kate Moss as a customer, you know that your stash of vintage costume and textiles is pretty much as good as it gets. This is vintage with an edge. There are no slightly smelly or scruffy goods here, just beautifully curated groupings of bygone style. Wedding dresses are a specialty (a gorgeous lace one from 1948 is £150), or flimsily sexy slips, vintage ribbons and trimmings, fur coats, even swimsuits. Rummage the rails and the quality is quickly apparent.

12 Camden Passage
N1 8ED
Tel 0207 359 0796
www.anniesvintageclothing.co.uk

4 ✳ LABOUR OF LOVE

The shop is testament to owner Francesca Forcolini's passion for offering something different to the usual high street shopping fare. A mix of own-label and independent designers, you'll find clothes, accessories, even the odd bit of taxidermy if it's taken Francesca's fancy. Her taste is on the quirky side, so if you want to wear something with a little bit of edge, she'll have it. Worth popping in just to admire the beautiful old premises. The gold leaf signage from the previous owner is still above the door, and the original desk and display cabinets continue to be used. Stunning 1960s light fittings complete the unique look and feel of the place.

193 Upper Street
N1 1RQ
Tel 0207 354 9333
www.labour-of-love.co.uk

'The owner has a passion for offering something different'

25

'No wonder Islingtonites can't imagine living anywhere else'

6✱

6✱ THE DRAPERS ARMS

Off the beaten track in one of Islington's most exclusive enclaves, this is the perfect neighbourhood pub. Forget images of a dark, smoky boozer, this is cool and chic from the minute you walk in. The elegant Georgian building boasts high, stencilled ceilings that create an open, airy feel to the room, while white tiling and shades of pale green on the walls add to the lightness. Seasonal menus change daily; dishes like whole Dorset crab with mayonnaise and salad and guinea fowl, bacon and prune pie put this in a different league to your average pint-and-packet-of-crisps watering hole. The annual December carol singing night is a locals' favourite.

44 Barnsbury Street
N1 1ER
Tel 0207 619 0348
www.thedrapersarms.com

7✱ THE ELK IN THE WOODS

With a look that's all its own, this quirky restaurant is a one-off worth seeing. Think hunting lodge meets antique shop. A stuffed stag's head takes pride of place, opposite a pink wall of vintage mirrors. Old ceramic tiling sits alongside quirkily modern wallpaper. It's slightly mad but it works. As for the food, from the breakfast bacon sarnie to the night-time small dishes of game pâté and chorizo and pancetta stew, there's a steady stream of treats to keep the crowds of locals happy.

39 Camden Passage
N1 8EA
Tel 0207 226 3535
www.the-elk-in-the-woods.co.uk

8✳ OTTOLENGHI

One of four cafés in the Ottolenghi empire, this is the biggest and the best. Abundance doesn't quite do it justice; the white, airy room is groaning with trays of exquisitely delicious-looking food. No other decoration is needed. Plump cherries sit on mini-cheesecakes, raspberries adorn lemon cupcakes, passionfruit meringues show off their perfect peaks. If you can tear your eyes away from the sweet goodies, the other side of the room tempts with Mediterranean-inspired savouries like roasted beetroot, and goat's cheese and onion marmalade tart. Mouth-watering.

287 Upper Street
N1 2TZ
0207 288 1454
www.ottolenghi.co.uk

9✳ THE DUKE OF CAMBRIDGE

Britain's first and only Soil Association certified gastro pub is not just one hundred per cent organic, it's also a stylish hideaway. Tucked down a leafy side street, if you didn't know it was there, you'd easily miss it. With menus that change twice daily to reflect what the suppliers have bought in (big multinationals and chain stores are shunned), the food is proudly sustainable and delicious. No wonder it's a repeated winner of the London Dining Pub of the Year. As for the design, the main room has the cool factor. Big wooden tables, mismatched chairs and funky green industrial light fittings. Definitely not your average pub.

30 St Peter's Street
N1 8JT
Tel 0207 359 3066
www.dukeorganic.co.uk

abigail ahern

*Interior designer, retailer, product designer and writer, Abigail Ahern is
multi-talented and hugely influential. As an interior designer her work has
included the Ritz Carlton's spa in Palm Beach, Florida, while her products,
such as her collection of lighting, are sold in Harrods and the Conran Shop.
But it's for her own shop Atelier Abigail Ahern that she's mainly known
and loved. An Aladdin's cave of interiors goodies, the walls are painted dark
(with Abigail's beloved London Clay shade from designer paint company,
Farrow & Ball), candles burn, and an abundance of buys fills every nook
and cranny. Choose from classic pieces like vases, cushions and throws,
or embrace Abigail's quirky chic taste with one of her own-designed
British bulldog lamps.*

ATELIER ABIGAIL AHERN
137 Upper Street N1 1QP ✾ **0207 354 8181** ✾ *www.atelierabigailahern.com*

'Parks inspire me, especially the Royal parks, watching the seasons change'

How would you define London style?

Edgy, experimental and innovative. I don't know whether it's because we live in such a cosmopolitan city or whether the weather makes us want to cheer ourselves up by being as creative as possible or a combo of both. Either way we love to mix and match, mingle vintage with high street and modern and use some high voltage doses of colour.

Where do you go in London to be inspired?

I walk a lot with my dog, so parks inspire me, especially the Royal parks, watching the seasons change. They constantly inspire with new interesting colour combinations. I also adore markets; Portobello, Borough and **Columbia Road** (see page 94).

Your favourite local places?

There are so many. **Violet** (see page 132) for the yummiest coffee and cakes—open the door and the most delicious smell of baking fills the air. Other local favourite places include **Broadway Market** (see page 125) every Saturday to stock up on groceries and wander around the cute stores.

31

Describe your perfect out-and-about weekend?

A drive to **Petersham Nurseries** (see page 280), parking in Richmond and strolling along the river to this beautiful nursery and Michelin-star restaurant. Then an afternoon spent wandering through Hyde Park and Green Park, ending up at Gordon's wine bar (www.gordonswinebar.com) for a late afternoon glass of wine. Sunday wouldn't be Sunday without a stroll to Columbia Road (see page 94) for flowers, brunch at **Brawn** (see page 111) or **Pizza East** (see page 159), a wander around Brick Lane (www.visitbricklane.org) and then home—usually via a drink at the **Cat & Mutton** (see page 130) with a big bundle of newspapers.

What's in your secret shopping address book?

For interiors, **Labour and Wait** in Redchurch Road (see page 153), **Fandango** (see page 21) in Islington for vintage and The Dog and Wardrobe (www.thedogandwardrobe.com) on Broadway Market. Then all the super sweet vintage clothes shops in Camden Passage. Go at the weekend and a tiny teeny market sets up there, too. Not forgetting **Nelly Duff** (see page 97) in Columbia Road for art.

Where's the best place for a weekend supper?

A Little of What You Fancy (www. alittleofwhatyoufancy.info) in a seedy bit of the Kingsland Road in Dalston, where I live. The food is fabulous and much of it comes from neighbourhood gardens—imagine organic roast rainbow trout with pink fir apple potatoes, or slow braised oxtail with red wine, herbs and garlic. Yummy.

Best place for a drink?

The bar at Moro (www.moro.co.uk) with a spot of tapas or the bar at Pizza East (see page 159) for people-watching.

Your favourite breakfast spot?

Towpath (see page 143) for cappuccino with granola, seasonal berries and yoghurt. They make everything from scratch. Or **E5 Bakehouse** (see page 119) under the arches in London Fields, where they bake and sell totally amazing bread.

Where do you go in London to relax?

I walk or I swim—Hyde Park, Green Park and Victoria Park are the lungs of our city and immediately relax me the moment I enter. Also, the outdoor pool at the bottom of my road, London Field's lido (www.hackney.gov.uk/c-londonfields-lido.htm). Nothing makes me feel better than a good swim outside.

Top 3 things that every visitor to London should do?

Borough Market (www.boroughmarket.org.uk) is a must to sample some of our fabulous British produce, drink coffee at Monmouth and then stroll along the river towards the Embankment. Wander around Shoreditch and Dalston—small stores, little cafés and art galleries abound. It's edgy and eclectic with a great vibe and for me pretty much personifies what London is all about. And the London Eye (www.londoneye.com) is a must for a bird's eye view of the city.

33

SHOP

1 *Mary's Living and Giving Shop*
2 *Bohemia*
3 *Shikasuki Vintage*
4 *Tann-Rokka*
5 *Primrose Bakery*
6 *Melrose and Morgan*

EAT & DRINK

7 *The Little One*
8 *The Lansdowne*

EAT, DRINK & SLEEP

9 *York & Albany*

● *Tube Station*

camden town

4

● *Chalk Farm*

Chalk Farm Rd

7

1

8

2

Gloucester Ave

5   3

6

Primrose Hill Rd

Regent's Park Rd

primrose hill

Prince Albert Rd

9

❋ LONDON ZOO ❋

primrose hill

north

Primrose Hill is shorthand for 'where London's A-listers live'. Jamie Oliver and his family reside in two knocked-together houses near the park, with singers Gwen Stefani, Gavin Rossdale and their sons just down the road. Rocker Noel Gallagher has moved on, but sold his mansion to Little Britain's David Walliams, so the celeb quota is still high. With its pretty streets and proximity to Regent's Park and central London, it's easy to see why it's one of the city's best-loved spots. Come and browse the shops then grab a coffee and hike up to the top of Primrose Hill for one of city's most romantic views. You'll be charmed.

1 ✳ MARY'S LIVING AND GIVING SHOP

British TV personality and retail guru Mary Portas has reinvented the traditional image of a fusty charity shop with her own-name outlets for Save the Children. Forget anything you thought about crammed rails of dodgy, unwanted items. Here, the space is curated like a treasure trove of clothes, books and homeware. The back is styled like a living room, with leather armchairs, wooden shelves of books and old Turkish rugs on the floor. At the front, a chandelier hangs over the rails of donated clothes. Comedian Ricky Gervais is among the high-profile shoppers you might spot in search of a bargain.

109 Regent's Park Road
NW1 8UR
Tel 0207 586 9966
www.savethechildren.org.uk

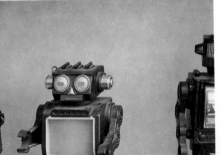

2✳ BOHEMIA

It's hard to know where to start describing this random mix of old toys, robots, bling 1960s lights, neon signage and modern artworks. Eclectic doesn't really cover it. It's less of a shop than a garage sale, with all the items unified by a slightly left-of-centre, rock 'n' roll sensibility. The owner is a huge fan of 1960s toy robots, hence the significant collection on offer, alongside 1980s Soho sex shop signs and portraits by local artists. Slightly bonkers, certainly; worth investigating, definitely.

156 Regent's Park Road
NW1 8XL
www.danielpoole.com

39

3 ✳ SHIKASUKI VINTAGE

Inside this all-white shop space, the vintage clothes stand out like brightly coloured jewels. It's a beautifully merchandised collection of labels, ranging from the seriously collectible like Ossie Clark and Bill Gibb, to the more fun and frivolous. Everything is in excellent condition, with any tiny defects marked on the labels, which also meticulously outline the item's date and fabric together with a 'helpful hint' on how to wear it. You'll want to stay and play among the rails of sequins and satins all day. It's the ultimate dressing-up box for grownups.

67 Gloucester Avenue
NW1 8LD
Tel 0207 722 4442
www.shikasuki.com

4 ✳ TANN-ROKKA

Do not miss this hoard of antique homeware and bespoke designs, crammed into what used to be the ticket office of Primrose Hill train station. The first thing to strike you is the mass of chandeliers hung the length of the narrow room. The effect is magical. The owner has classic taste with a twist. Mirrored and more traditional pieces of furniture sit alongside deer antlers painted and studded with Swarovski crystals—a favourite with the local A-listers. When you've had your fill, cross the street and see if the shop's tea garden is open; its hours are seasonal and weekends only. With tables set in a hidden garden of lavender, geraniums and tubs of herbs, it's a secret getaway for a cup of mint tea (picked from the garden, of course) and slice of homemade cake.

123 Regent's Park Road
NW1 8BE
Tel 0207 722 3999
www.tannrokka.com

5✳ PRIMROSE BAKERY

With its sunny canary yellow frontage, pale green walls and strings of bunting hanging over the counter, this gorgeous cupcake specialist is a very happy place to be. Trays of mouth-watering cakes are lined up in the counter cabinet—and not just any old flavours. Choose from the likes of peanut butter or delicately pale mauve Earl Grey, then sit at one of the 1950s Formica tables with a cup of tea and enjoy.

69 Gloucester Avenue
NW1 8LD
Tel 0207 483 4222
www.primrosebakery.org.uk

7✳ THE LITTLE ONE

It's worth walking to the far end of Regent's Park Road, away from the shops, to find this tiny coffee hangout. Tucked into the old office space of the antique shop next door—the vintage lights are for sale, courtesy of the neighbours—it's a chic retreat from the bustle of the rest of the street. The house specialities are crêpes (calorie-conscious locals love the spinach and carrot versions) and homemade breads. Most things are sold out by 2 pm.

115 Regent's Park Road
NW1 8UR

8 ✳ THE LANSDOWNE

Why can't every neighbourhood have a local pub like the Lansdowne? The airy main room is everything you want a laid-back drinking and eating destination to be. With big wooden tables, a lovely old pressed-plaster ceiling, metal jugs of flowers on the counter and a blackboard menu, it's hard to think of a better place for a lazy weekend afternoon. Unfussy and with great food; the perfect combination.

90 Gloucester Avenue
NW1 8HX
Tel 0207 483 0409
www.thelansdownepub.co.uk

9 ✳ YORK & ALBANY

This elegant pub, restaurant and hotel, part of Gordon Ramsay's empire, occupies an 1820s, Grade II listed, John Nash-designed building on the edge of Regent's Park. It's a very civilised spot for a stop-off. Pop in for just breakfast or a coffee before hitting the Primrose Hill shops, or for a drink and dinner at the end of the day. The lovely main bar has high ceilings with intricate cornicing, parquet floors and a long stainless steel bar topped with huge flower arrangements. Settle back into one of the elegant grey velvet armchairs and relax. Overnight guests are well looked after in gorgeous rooms kitted out with chandeliers, gilt mirrors, old Turkish carpets and some of the most comfortable mattresses in London. Before you leave, duck into Nonna's Deli next door. Created in the building's original stables, its rough brick floor and rustic charms offset the smart main building beautifully. And the takeaway coffee is great.

127–129 Parkway
NW1 7PS
Tel 0207 387 5700
www.gordonramsay.com

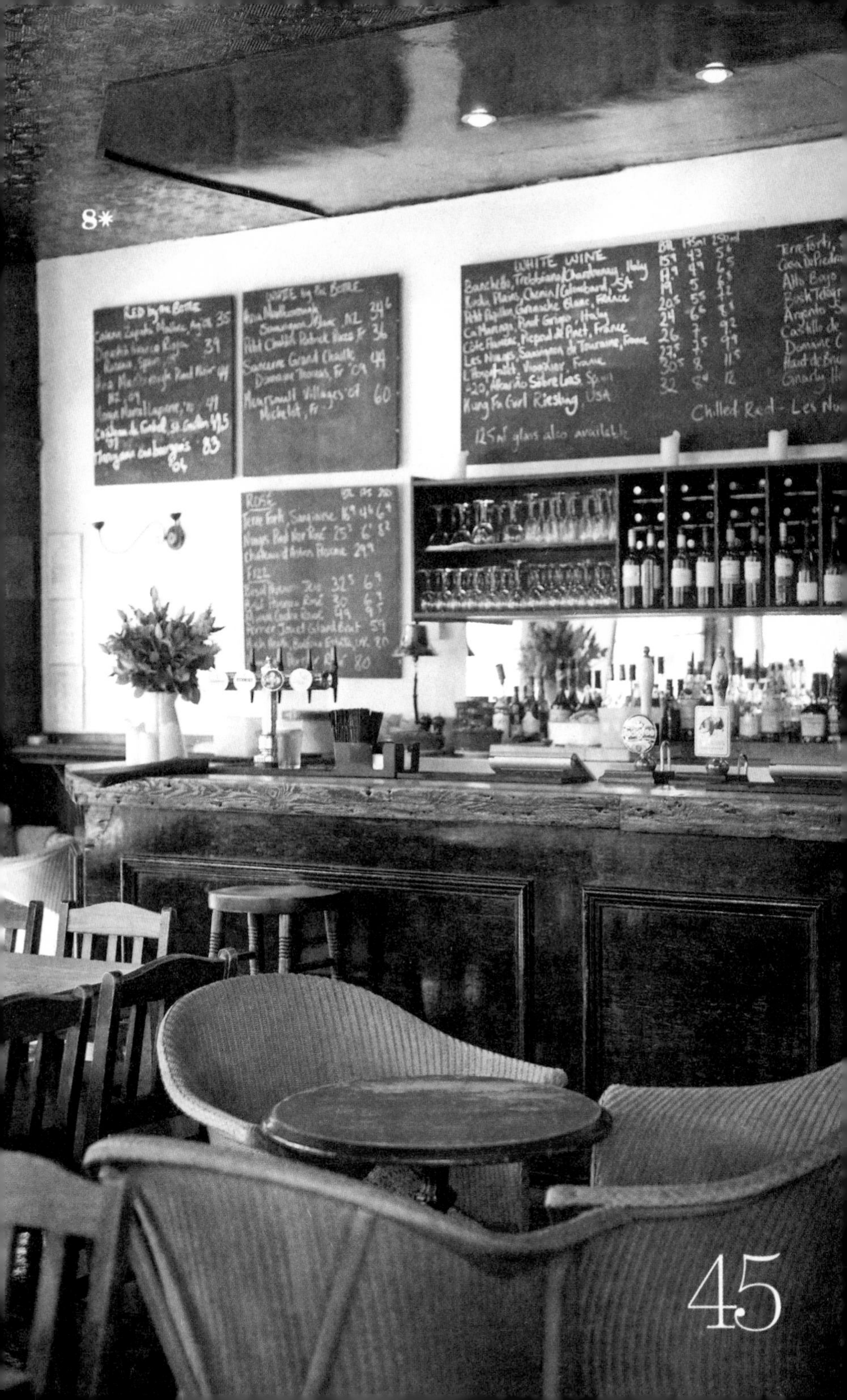
8*
WHITE WINE
125ml glass also available
45

nick selby
& ian james

Far too stylish to be called just a grocer's, Melrose and Morgan is a deli cum café cum kitchen that's a foodie's heaven. Not only are owners Nick Selby and Ian James passionate about food, but they have CVs that encompass photography, fashion and theatre, which explains the shop's stylish, visual appeal. Set in a funky modern space of bricks and glass, it's crammed with temptations. A table is piled high with homemade cakes like cherry pies and giant meringues, while the fridge is stocked with home-baked pies that even come in their own baking tin (so you can pass them off as your own!). Pop in for a coffee and leave with a jar of local Regent's Park honey.

Melrose and Morgan
42 Gloucester Avenue ❀ **NW1 8JD** ❀ **0207 722 0011** ❀ *www.melroseandmorgan.com*

'We love seeing
art and films,
especially at
the Barbican'

How would you define London style?

It's diverse just by the nature of all the different age groups, professions, cultures and nationalities that live here.

Where do you go in London to be inspired?

It used to be art galleries and photographic exhibitions. Nowadays it's a trip to Selfridges food hall (www.selfridges.com), to keep up with food trends or a trip to Borough Market (www.boroughmarket.org. uk) and **Maltby Street** (see page 50) to see what's on offer south of the river. We still love seeing art and films though, especially at the Barbican (www.barbican.org.uk).

Your favourite local places?

Our friend Claire Ptak runs **Violet** (see page 132) around the corner from where we live in London Fields. She sells great coffee from Colemans and the ginger bread is delicious—we are addicted.

47

Describe your perfect out-and-about weekend?

We work most weekends, as it's our busiest time. But it would definitely involve supper with friends on Saturday night at **Pizza East** (see page 159) then a walk through **Columbia Road Flower Market** (see page 94) on Sunday, then down Brick Lane (www.visitbricklane.org) and into Spitalfields Market (www.spitalfields. co.uk) for a browse. We usually end up at the Whitechapel Gallery (www. whitechapelgallery.org) for some culture and a bite to eat.

What's in your secret shopping address book?

For clothes, Albam in Islington (www.albamclothing.com); the clothes are very well made and they use interesting fabrics. For food, Leila's Grocery Shop in Shoreditch (15–17 Calvert Avenue, E2 7JP. Tel 0207 729 9789). It's the best food shop in London: fantastic breads, wonderful cured meats from Poland and a superb selection of vegetables. For the bathroom, Aesop in Shoreditch (www.aesop.com), especially for its geranium shower gel; and for books, **Daunt Books** on Marylebone High Street (see page 217). We love this old-fashioned bookshop and it's on our favourite high street.

Where's the best place for a weekend supper?

For a treat we would go to The Boundary (www.theboundary.co.uk). It's in the basement but still has huge high ceilings studded with old silver serving trays; very theatrical. The service is impeccable and the roast sirloin beef is the best in town. Then for something more casual, we will queue for our supper at **Spuntino** in Soho (see page 274) or the excellent grill at Barrafina, also in Soho (www.barrafina. co.uk); both are well worth the wait.

Best place for a drink?

The bar at **St John** on St John Street (see page 81). They also serve great bar snacks like smoked sprats with horseradish and the best cheese on toast.

Your favourite breakfast spot?

The bacon sandwich at St John Bread and Wine in Spitalfields (www. stjohnbreadandwine.com) should not be missed, followed by a custard doughnut, if you can fit one in.

Where do you go in London to relax?

A walk through Regent's Park normally does the trick.

Top three things that every visitor to London should do?

See some great art at the Tate Modern (www.tate.org.uk) then a walk over the Millennium Bridge to St Paul's (www. stpauls.co.uk) and visit the Whispering Gallery. Then have lunch in nearby Clerkenwell at The Modern Pantry (www.themodernpantry.co.uk) where Anna Hanson serves up brilliantly tasty fusion food all day long.

49

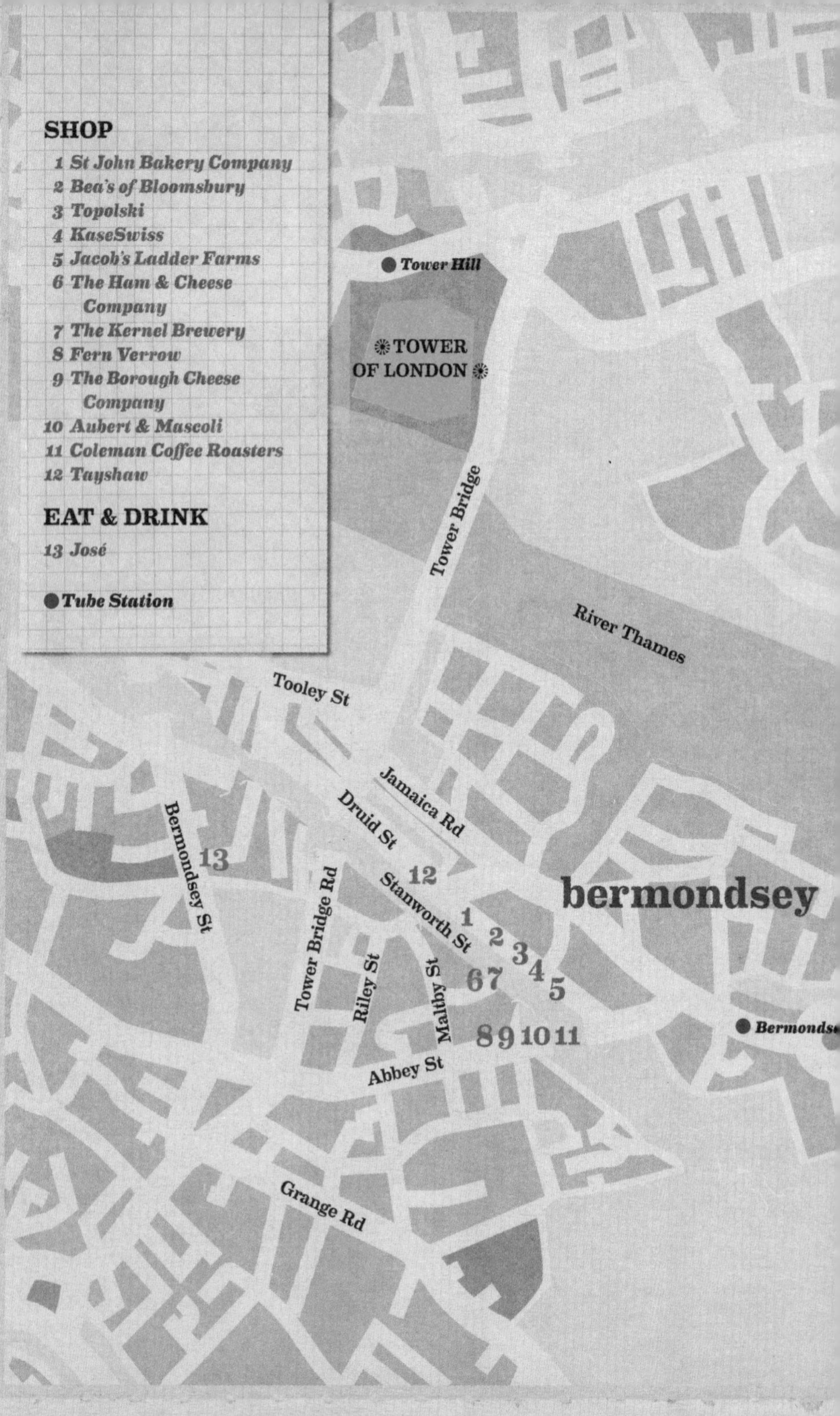

SHOP

1 *St John Bakery Company*
2 *Bea's of Bloomsbury*
3 *Topolski*
4 *KaseSwiss*
5 *Jacob's Ladder Farms*
6 *The Ham & Cheese Company*
7 *The Kernel Brewery*
8 *Fern Verrow*
9 *The Borough Cheese Company*
10 *Aubert & Mascoli*
11 *Coleman Coffee Roasters*
12 *Tayshaw*

EAT & DRINK

13 *José*

● *Tube Station*

● Tower Hill

❋ TOWER OF LONDON ❋

Tower Bridge

River Thames

Tooley St

Jamaica Rd

Druid St

Bermondsey St

Tower Bridge Rd

Riley St

Stanworth St

Maltby St

12

bermondsey

13

1 2 3 4 5
6 7
8 9 10 11

● Bermonds

Abbey St

Grange Rd

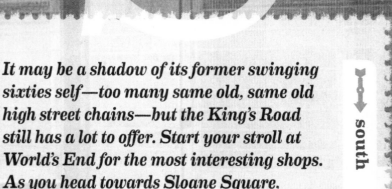

chelsea & south kensington

It may be a shadow of its former swinging sixties self—too many same old, same old high street chains—but the King's Road still has a lot to offer. Start your stroll at World's End for the most interesting shops. As you head towards Sloane Square, things become a bit more predictable. Better to take a detour into nearby South Kensington, with its beautifully leafy residential streets and pockets of interesting shops. This is one of the most polished areas of London and just meandering around its streets is a lovely way to spend an afternoon. Think of it as lifestyle window-shopping.

1✱ ROCOCO CHOCOLATES

Opened in 1983, this chocoholics' paradise
was one of the first purveyors of the kind
of luxury, unusual chocolates that are
now commonplace, but no one does it
better than Rococo. And no one has a
prettier shop. Old botanical prints adorn
the walls, a chandelier hangs from the
ceiling and trays of handmade delicacies
are displayed in an old-fashioned cabinet.
Elsewhere, shelves are stacked with
gorgeously wrapped bars with flavours
like orange and geranium dark milk and
sea salt milk chocolate, while pretty,
ribboned boxes are stacked on a dresser.
One hundred per cent temptation.
321 King's Road
SW3 5EP
Tel 0207 352 5857
www.rococochocolates.com

2✱ GREEN AND STONE

A Chelsea institution, Green and Stone
has been selling art materials here since
1934. Whether you're an amateur or a
professional, it's a pleasure just to browse
the crammed shelves. Old plan chests are
filled with any and every type of paper;
you'll find gold leaf, paints, pencils—
whatever your creative heart desires.
The shop itself is given a delightfully
higgledy-piggledy atmosphere by the
sloping worn wood floors and piled-high
merchandise. If anywhere is going to
inspire you to get creative, this place is it.
259 King's Road
SW3 5EL
Tel 0207 351 1098
www.greenandstone.com

3❋ FEW AND FAR

Visiting here is always an experience, with its constantly shifting merchandise and one-off exhibits. An imaginative mix of homeware and fashion, the taste is eclectic and inspiring. A selection of French children's toys is displayed alongside a goldfish candle, which sits on a pricey polished aluminium table. Clothes from as far afield as Mongolia and as close to home as the UK are hung with striking pieces of jewellery and accessories. Down the other end of the room, a display of twentieth-century collectible glassware creates an art gallery feel. The window displays never disappoint—it's not often you see a space filled with a huge pile of sand and hammocks strung up to create a holiday atmosphere.

242 Brompton Road
SW3 2BB
Tel 0207 225 7070
www.fewandfar.net

4❋ SIGMAR

The owner's single-minded passion for beautifully made, classic furniture shines through in this small, sleek shop. The stock is from a mix of eras, but it's unified by its simple, tasteful style. Nineteenth-century wooden chairs sit alongside twenty-first-century light fittings and perfectly crafted oak tables that were designed fifty years ago but look modern today. No clutter, just a careful edit of very good taste, set against the shop's pale grey walls and polished wood floor. Lovely.

236 King's Road
SW3 5EL
Tel 0207 751 5801
www.sigmarlondon.com

5✳ DESIGNERS GUILD

If your taste in homeware tends towards minimalism, then step away from this shop. If however, you love colour, pattern and vibrancy, come on in. Every surface is decorated with stripes, flowers and geometric designs and you can't help but be put in a positive mood. Blended in with the home accessories are handpicked pieces of vintage furniture, like a 1950s chair reupholstered in bold green tweed or an old teak side table with a bright yellow laminated top. The mix of old and new is perfectly judged. If you're not a colour convert by the time you leave, then you never will be.

267–277 King's Road
SW3 5EN
Tel 0207 351 5775
www.designersguild.com

8✳ THE CONRAN SHOP

Housed in the decorative 1909 building that was once the HQ of the Michelin Tyre Company, this has to be one of London's most impressive shop settings. There's world class furniture shopping inside, or just visit for a glass of Champagne and a platter of *fruits de mer* in the oyster bar, which bears the same name as the iconic cheekily chubby Michelin Man, Monsieur Bibendum. Set in the shop's beautifully tiled forecourt, it's an elegant spot to rest after a hard day's shopping. The florist at the front of the building has to be one of the prettiest flower stalls in town.

Michelin House
81 Fulham Road
SW3 6RD
Tel 0207 589 7401
www.conranshop.co.uk

6✱ THE SHOP AT BLUEBIRD

Housed in a cavernous Art Deco garage, this lifestyle shop is a seductive blend of high-end designer and quirky, affordable buys. It's hard to think where else a tube of cinnamon toothpaste would be displayed alongside a £1800 YSL dress. It's a magical mix. The space itself is worth a look; it's huge. Enter through a café on the old garage forecourt and you're into a warehouse-sized room of womenswear, menswear, antique furnishings, books, magazines, artworks—and the odd tube of toothpaste. There's even a spa. Get your eyebrows threaded or spend £3800 on an antique French mirror, the choice is yours.
350 King's Road
SW3 5UU
Tel 0207 351 3873
www.theshopatbluebird.com

7✱ VICTORIA & ALBERT MUSEUM CAFÉ

It may be one of the world's great museums, but the V&A also has a hidden secret—one of London's most ornate cafés. Not just that, it was the first museum restaurant in the world, built in the 1860s to show off British design and craftsmanship. As entry to the museum is free, you can come for coffee at the V&A without feeling you ought to check out the art, although the glorious Victorian decor in the café is an experience in itself. There are three rooms to choose from: Morris, Gamble and Poynter. In the Morris room, created by designer William Morris's decorating company, you'll find theatrical stained glass and wonderfully tiled sweeping arches. In Gamble, the walls are covered in ceramic tiles and the ceiling in enamelled iron, all richly patterned and ornate. The Poynter room's colour scheme of blue and white is inspired by Dutch artists. London's most OTT coffee stop.
Cromwell Road
SW7 2RL
Tel 0207 942 2000
www.vam.ac.uk

kit kemp

Hotelier Kit Kemp is the woman behind some of London's best boutique hotels. Together with her husband Tim she owns Firmdale Hotels, with six London establishments and construction of a seventh underway just behind Piccadilly. Her touch is unmistakeable: an intoxicating and playful blend of art, colour and pattern, combined with the highest levels of luxury and service. No wonder her creations, including the Soho, Covent Garden and Charlotte Street hotels, are some of the most popular in the capital. Number Sixteen is the most bijou of the group, tucked into a Victorian terraced house in a residential street. A short stroll from the Victoria & Albert and Natural History Museums, as well as from the shops of Knightsbridge and the greenery of Kensington Gardens, it's also blessed with one of London's prettiest hotel gardens. The perfect place to stay.

Number Sixteen
16 Sumner Place SW7 3EG ❧ **Tel 0207 589 5232** ❧ *www.firmdale.com*

'I love ballet and the old Covent Garden Market with its street entertainment'

How would you define London style?
English eccentric.

Where do you go in London to be inspired?
London is like a collection of villages and I am part of South Kensington where I live, with all its beautiful white stucco buildings. I like the fact that London is so green with its many parks. I walk to work everyday from home, which is near the Royal Albert Hall (www.royalalberthall.com). I always go down Exhibition Road, past the Science Museum (www.sciencemuseum.org.uk) and the Natural History Museum (www.nhm.ac.uk), which is my favourite building in London.

Your favourite local places?
Few and Far (see page 66). I love the vintage and contemporary furniture, especially the pieces by Paola Navone. The Victoria & Albert Reading rooms (www.vandareadingrooms.co.uk) and Mint (www.mintshop.co.uk)—a great shop where you can always find something different and quirky.

Describe your perfect out-and-about weekend?

I go to the country every weekend, but if I was in London then it would involve walking around the Covent Garden area, including Long Acre and Neal Street for the different shops and street life, going to the Royal Opera House (www.roh.org.uk) as I love ballet, and the old Covent Garden Market with its street entertainment and attractions.

What's in your secret shopping address book?

Talisman (www.talismanlondon.com) for a fabulous selection of unique mid-twentieth-century furniture and eighteenth-century continental antiques. Tissus d'Hélène at Chelsea Harbour (www.tissusdhelene.co.uk) for designer fabrics and wallpapers from Europe and America. Bloomsbury Flowers (www.bloomsburyflowers.co.uk) put together some of the most beautiful flower arrangements in London. The owners are both ex-Royal Ballet School dancers and supply the flowers for the Royal Opera House. And St Paul's (www.actorschurch.org) has wonderful Orpheus Foundation concerts and recitals.

Where's the best place for a weekend supper?

Brasserie Max at the Covent Garden Hotel. Or for a very simple meal, Ikeda (30 Brook Street, W1K 5DJ. Tel 0207 629 2730 www.ikedarestaurant.co.uk), my favourite Japanese restaurant in London. I love sitting at the counter watching them cook exquisite things.

Best place for a drink?

I love the Rose Bakery in **Dover Street Market** (see page 282) for tea and carrot cake.

Your favourite breakfast spot?

The café at the Serpentine (www.serpentinebarandkitchen.com) in Hyde Park, as I like to watch the swimmers in the morning.

Favourite cultural London sights?

The Royal Opera House (I love going to the ballet not only for the amazing performances but for the beautiful building and wonderful sets), the Sir John Soane's Museum (www.soane.org), and the Wallace Collection (www.wallacecollection.org).

Top three things that every visitor to London should do?

Take a Boris Bike (London's cycle rental scheme, nicknamed for the city's mayor, www.tfl.gov.uk) to the Tate Modern (www.tate.org.uk), and then cycle along the South Bank and pop over the bridge to Somerset House (www.somersethouse.org.uk), where you can ice skate in the winter or look at the art and cultural exhibitions. Pack a picnic to have in St James's Park. And go to the Royal Opera House and watch ballet or an opera and have a very relaxed supper in the Paul Hamlyn Hall to look at all the surroundings in the interval.

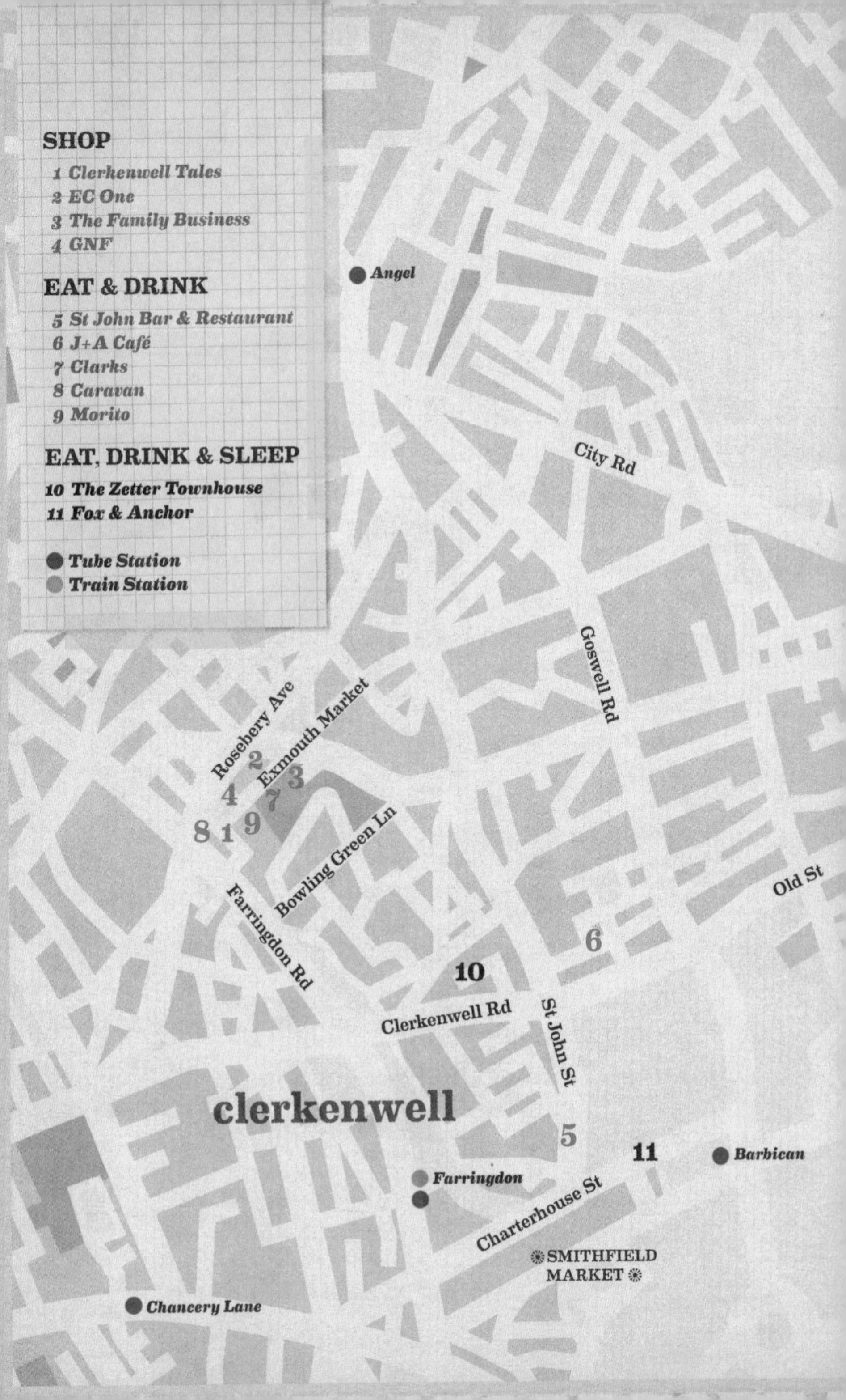

SHOP

1 Clerkenwell Tales
2 EC One
3 The Family Business
4 GNF

EAT & DRINK

5 St John Bar & Restaurant
6 J+A Café
7 Clarks
8 Caravan
9 Morito

EAT, DRINK & SLEEP

10 The Zetter Townhouse
11 Fox & Anchor

● Tube Station
● Train Station

● Angel

City Rd

Goswell Rd

Rosebery Ave

Exmouth Market

2
4 3
8 1 9 7

Bowling Green Ln

Farringdon Rd

Old St

6

10

Clerkenwell Rd

St John St

clerkenwell

5

● Farringdon

11

● Barbican

Charterhouse St

❋ SMITHFIELD
MARKET ❋

● Chancery Lane

clerkenwell

From the Grade II listed Victorian splendour of Smithfield meat market through history-soaked cobbled squares and laneways to the pedestrianised charm of Exmouth Market, this is one of the most picturesque pockets of London. Clerkenwell has been a hub of activity since the Middle Ages, when the clerks (clergymen) put on mystery plays at the site of the Clerks' Well in Farringdon Lane. These days, you're more likely to find architects, interior designers and other cool creatives, who gather at the area's many pubs and restaurants. But the cobbles are still there, as are many of the medieval buildings. If you love urban history, it's a part of London not to be missed.

1✳ CLERKENWELL TALES

Times are tough for the book trade so this independently owned shop is a rarity. The owner prides himself on his careful edit of fiction, art and design, culture and politics, and London writing. The shop also specialises in distinctively beautiful books, especially graphic novels, curating them like treasures on the shop's streamlined shelves. No wonder David *One Day* Nicholls regularly pops in for a browse.

30 Exmouth Market
EC1R 4QE
Tel 0207 713 8135
www.clerkenwell-tales.co.uk

2✳ EC ONE

This independent jewellery shop champions new designers as well as creating bespoke pieces in its on-site workshop. The result is a range that goes above and beyond your average jewellery shop, with items from the cheap and quirky up to the grandly precious. The passion for good design is clear, with a constant stream of undiscovered names showcased in the shop's annual graduate design awards. You'll definitely find something unusually special here.

41 Exmouth Market
EC1R 4QL
Tel 0207 243 8811
www.econe.co.uk

4✳ GNF

Eleven-year-old dachshund Ron stands guard in the doorway of this mid-century furniture paradise. Ron's owner Nikolaus Greig is the man responsible for an exceedingly tempting collection of English and Scandinavian design classics. From vintage fabric cushions and ceramics to glassware and larger pieces of furniture, this small shop packs a punch.
60 Exmouth Market
EC1R 4QE
Tel 0207 833 0370
www.gnfurniture.co.uk

5✳ ST JOHN BAR AND RESTAURANT

One of the first businesses to move in and turn Clerkenwell into the don't-miss destination it is today, St John is also one of London's most cutting edge restaurants. It frequently tops the lists of chefs' own favourite places to eat. Nose-to-tail dining is the philosophy in this former ham and bacon smokehouse. Go for the whole roast suckling pig to get the full experience. Decor is white, stripped-back and industrial looki   re like a photographer's studio   most revered restaura   if you just pop in for a   don't miss it.
26 St John Street
EC1M 4AY
Tel 0203 301 8069
www.stjohnrestaur

1 sml pie and mash £3·50
1 lge pie and mash £3·60
2 sml pie and mash £5·50
2 lge pie and mash £5·70

eels and mash £4-10
jellied eels £2·60
HOT EELS £2·75

MUG TEA 95p
MUG COFFEE £1

Soft DRINKS - 85p

6*

6*

7*

7*

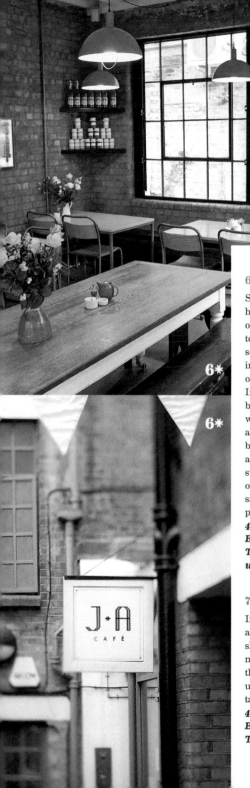

6✳ J+A CAFÉ

Sisters Aoife and Johanna Ledwidge have created a secret café oasis in this old diamond-cutting factory. You have to be in the know to find it but it's worth seeking out. Walk down an alleyway and into a shady courtyard filled with tubs of geraniums and hung with bunting. Inside, exposed brick walls, an oversized blackboard and a large communal wooden table create a relaxed, friendly atmosphere. As for the food, soda bread and cakes are homemade daily and ingredients are sourced from local suppliers where possible. If in doubt over the menu, order the roast chicken sandwich on white crusty bread; it's pretty unbeatable.

4 Sutton Lane
EC1M 5PU
Tel 0207 490 2992
www.jandacafe.com

7✳ CLARKS

If pie, mash and possibly jellied eels are your thing, then this traditional pie shop is the place to get them. Pretty much unchanged since its 1910 opening, this basic tiled eatery is a little piece of unreconstructed east London. Come and taste a bit of cockney history.

46 Exmouth Market
EC1R 4QE
Tel 0207 837 1974

9*

9*

8* CARAVAN

A great coffee is guaranteed at this busy corner café. Beans are roasted on-site to create one of the best cups in the capital, but don't come just for the coffee. Join the crowds who have made Caravan one of London's favourite brunch spots, thanks to its spot-on menu ('two crumpets and too much butter'), cool decor and always-friendly staff. Dinner is also worth a look. With its rough concrete floor, reclamation wood bar and huge glass industrialesque lights, the whole place has a funky, laid-back feel that makes for the perfect weekend morning of paper-reading and people-watching.
11–13 Exmouth Market
EC1R 4QD
Tel 0207 833 8115
www.caravanonexmouth.co.uk

9* MORITO

London's hippest tapas bar is the rough-and-ready younger sibling of Moro restaurant next door, and brings a little slice of Spain to east London. With the tiny space dominated by an orange Formica counter and a few tables and stools (no comfy dining chairs here), the look is no-frills but the food is anything but. The place is always packed with diners enjoying wine by the carafe and food that takes your breath away. Don't be put off by the strip lighting. This is one of the most delicious spots in the area.
32 Exmouth Market
EC1R 4QL
Tel 0207 278 7007

8*

85

10✷ THE ZETTER TOWNHOUSE

The cocktail bar of this thirteen-bedroom Georgian townhouse hotel is the perfect place to begin or end an evening—or both. Tucked at the back of a cobbled square, there's no clue from the outside to the fantastical atmosphere within. Cross the threshold and you're into Dickens' *The Old Curiosity Shop*. Part apothecary, part gentleman's club, the bar is filled with potted palms, stag antlers, taxidermy, old framed prints and worn Turkish rugs. Settle back in a velvet Chesterfield sofa or sink into an armchair upholstered with an old hessian sack. Then order a cocktail that nods to the area's Dickensian past of gin distilleries and debauchery. The martini even comes with a homemade citrus essence, dispensed into your drink with a glass pipette by the waiter. As for the bedrooms, they are sexy, fun and bijoux. Old fairground carousel signage is used as bedheads, there's boldly striped carpet, brightly painted walls and glam touches of gold mosaic tiling. It all makes for a very theatrical night out.

49–50 St John's Square
EC1V 4JJ
Tel 0207 324 4567
www.thezettertownhouse.com

87

11✴ FOX & ANCHOR

This pub with six bedrooms upstairs
is a jewel of Victoriana. Beautifully
restored, it's a perfect example of what
a proper London boozer—as opposed
to a tricked-up gastro pub—should be.
The mahogany panelling, Arts and Crafts
era tiling, etched glass and moulded
decorative ceiling create a room that
has character in abundance. Sit up at
the bar and wash down a homemade pork
pie with a pint of London ale from an
antique pewter tankard, or venture to the
Fox's Den at the back of the pub, where
dining tables are tucked away in their own
cosy wood-panelled rooms. After a dinner
of traditional British fare (homemade
pies, oysters, perfectly cooked steak) you
can venture upstairs to one of the elegant
bedrooms. Soak in an oversized bath and
then crawl into a supremely comfortable
bed. One tip: take earplugs. The downside
of a night in the heart of one of London's
hippest neighbourhoods is the sound of
its trendy young things partying the night
away. Not even double glazing on the
original lead windows can fix that.
115 Charterhouse Street
EC1M 6AA
Tel 0207 250 1300
www.foxandanchor.com

'After a dinner of traditional British fare (homemade pies, oysters, perfectly cooked steak) you can venture upstairs to one of the elegant bedrooms'

89

mo coppoletta

*Prepare to have all your preconceived ideas about tattoo parlours challenged.
In The Family Business, the tattoo is treated as a twenty-first-century art
form. Step into a world of religious iconography, hand-painted framed design
illustrations and artists' portfolios, where the gentle hum of tattooing needles
comes from the studio at the back. Italian-born owner Mo Coppoletta—
creator of this temple to the tattoo—has recently collaborated with artist
Damien Hirst, and credits an early exposure to religious and decorative art
with drawing him into the tattoo business. Peruse the portfolios to choose
your artist, who will then create a bespoke design, just for you. It's a serious
business: you can book one of the many visiting international practitioners
who view a stint here as a rite of passage, but if you want to wait for Mo
himself, join the year-long queue.*

THE FAMILY BUSINESS
58 Exmouth Market EC1R 4QE ❋ **0207 278 9526** ❋ *www.thefamilybusinesstattoo.com*

> 'I love paintings and nothing is more inspiring than the National Gallery'

How would you define London style?

It's fresh and innovative but timeless at the same time.

Where do you go in London to be inspired?

The National Portrait Gallery (www. npg.org.uk), The National Gallery (www. nationalgallery.org.uk) and Estorick Collection of Modern Italian Art (www. estorickcollection.com). I love paintings and nothing is more inspiring than selecting a couple of rooms at the National Gallery and immersing myself in a few selected works at a time. Portraits are always so direct and pure. They have a lot of power. That's why I love the National Portrait Gallery. I'm also a big fan of the futurist movement and Italian art from the first half of the twentieth century and the Estorick Collection is the perfect place for it.

Your favourite local places to eat?

Bistro du Vin (www.bistroduvinandbar.com, see page 270) and The Eagle in Clerkenwell (159 Farringdon Road, EC1R 3AL. Tel 0207

837 1353). Bistro is the number one for meat and oysters, their tartare is to die for, the ambience is very cosy and the wine list is terrific. I discovered The Eagle only recently and wondered how I could have left the first-ever gastro pub off my list of places for so long. Go for their signature steak sandwich.

What's in your secret shopping address book?

It's no secret—Saville Row in Mayfair. Spencer Hart (www.spencerhart.com) for his 1960s inspired tailoring and Lanvin (www.lanvin.com) all around.

Describe your perfect out-and-about weekend?

A stroll down to the South Bank Centre (www.southbankcentre.co.uk), or a jog in Hyde Park followed by a visit to the Serpentine (www.serpentinegallery.org) and dinner in one of the restaurants mentioned below.

Where's the best place for a weekend supper?

Roka (www.rokarestaurant.com) for oriental atmosphere, La Petite Maison (www.lpmlondon.co.uk) for a breeze of the French Riviera or L'Anima (www.lanima.co.uk) for the finest Italian.

Best place for a drink?

The Connaught Bar (www.the-connaught.co.uk) for its sleek decor and exquisite drinks (the Bloody Mary is amazing) or 69 Colebrooke Row (www.69colebrookerow.com), which is London's best-kept secret. Here you can enjoy arguably the best drinks in the world. My friend Tony (the owner) is a genius.

Your favourite breakfast spot?

A good start to the day is an Italian cappuccino at Cecconi's (www.cecconis.co.uk) in Mayfair.

93

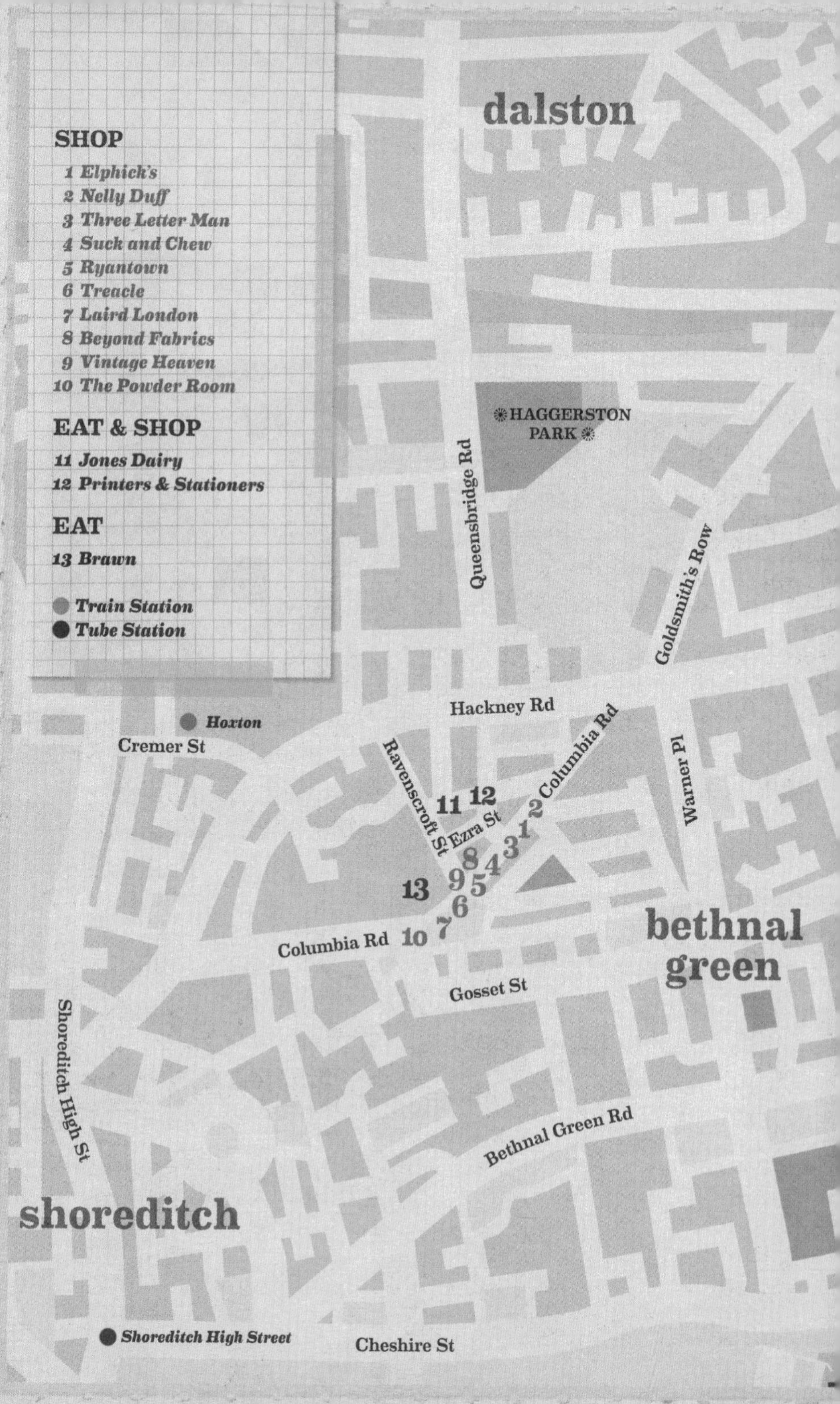

SHOP

1 Elphick's
2 Nelly Duff
3 Three Letter Man
4 Suck and Chew
5 Ryantown
6 Treacle
7 Laird London
8 Beyond Fabrics
9 Vintage Heaven
10 The Powder Room

EAT & SHOP

11 Jones Dairy
12 Printers & Stationers

EAT

13 Brawn

● Train Station
● Tube Station

dalston

HAGGERSTON PARK

Queensbridge Rd

Goldsmith's Row

Hackney Rd

Hoxton

Cremer St

Ravenscroft St

Ezra St

Columbia Rd

Warner Pl

11 12
8 4 3 2
9 5
13
6
10 7

Columbia Rd

Gosset St

bethnal green

Shoreditch High St

Bethnal Green Rd

shoreditch

● Shoreditch High Street

Cheshire St

In an age of chain stores and lookalike high streets, Columbia Road is a magical spot. This tiny strip of independent shops comes alive only at weekends—some of the shops are Sunday-only, when a flower market down the middle of the road draws the crowds, others open Saturday and Sunday, too. Call each shop individually to check their hours. On Sunday it gets very busy, but it's worth the squash. Come early and just wander, grabbing a coffee and some flowers along the way.

1*

1

2*

2

1❋ELPHICK'S

Quirky and whimsical are the best words to describe the aesthetic of the art on show in this print shop set up by artist–owner Sharon Elphick. Her own distinctive work is displayed alongside the likes of wildlife artist Charley Harper; Elphick's is Harper's only UK stockist and his charmingly colourful and distinctive pictures sum up the vibe of the place. A deliberately non-gallery-like mood has been created by displaying the art on items found at car boot sales and markets. If a picture doesn't tempt you, then a tea towel, cushion cover, book or handmade greeting card is sure to.

160 Columbia Road
E2 7RG
Tel 0207 033 7891
www.elphicksshop.com

2❋NELLY DUFF

There's a dark sense of humour running through many of the works on show in this gallery—like a portrait of Che Guevara fashioned from logos of the US firms who have turned a tidy profit in Cuba. Edgy and just-provocative-enough, the gallery name is emblazoned in bold lights across the shop front, while inside the art hangs on exposed brick walls. All budgets are catered for, with many pieces created exclusively for here. It will be hard to leave empty-handed.

156 Columbia Road
E2 7RG
Tel 0207 033 9683
www.nellyduff.com

3❋ THREE LETTER MAN

If you spot a figure sitting casually on a first floor window sill, happily stitching away at embroidery while wearing a giant fox head mask, it will be artist Nathan Hanford. Go up and see him. His tiny studio, reached by a rickety flight of stairs, is a secret space well worth checking out. In among shelves piled with vintage linen and artwork (such as a mass of old scissors mounted in a picture frame), you'll find Nathan's distinctive hand-embroidered artwork— explicit images, disconcertingly rendered in spindly black thread. The fox head is a beautifully hand-crocheted mask made by an artist friend of Nathan's.

146A Columbia Road
E2 7RG
Tel 07912 619 226
www.threeletterman.com

4❋ SUCK AND CHEW

Remember the excitement you felt when visiting your local sweet shop as a kid? You can relive it here. This is everything a confectioner's should be, a joyous riot of sugary treats and sticky indulgences. Jars of sweets are measured out by hand into red and white stripy paper bags. Old-fashioned tins are packed with toffees. Retro mugs from the Queen's Coronation and Silver Jubilee are filled to the brim. A handwritten blackboard announces that 'salty liquorice is back in'. And to complete the mood, vintage toys, school satchels and Ladybird books are used as decorations, with a string of Union Jack bunting hung over the shop counter. Release your inner eight-year-old and enjoy.

130 Columbia Road
E2 7RG
0208 983 3504
www.suckandchew.co.uk

99

5✳RYANTOWN

Artist Rob Ryan sells his exquisite hand-cut paper prints around the world, but this is his only dedicated shop. His studio is just around the corner, and much of the work sold here is exclusive. If you don't know his style, prepare to be enchanted. Whimsical, romantic and a little bit kooky, his pictures feature sayings ('Let your heart have a say', 'I miss being a small girl') that will have you smiling and feeling fuzzy around the edges. The shop itself is utterly charming. With lovely worn floorboards, hand-stencilled tiles and tea towels imploring you to 'Believe in People', it's a world of traditional manners and romantic daydreams. Just lovely.

126 Columbia Road
E2 6QE
www.misterrob.co.uk

101

6 ✴ TREACLE

It's hard to think of a better name for
a shop that celebrates all things cakey.
Reminiscent of postwar London teashops
like Lyons and focused on good honest
baking, the mood is homely rather than
twee—a world away from the too-sugary
cake shops that proliferate today. Vintage
1950s kitchen units are stacked high with
cooking paraphernalia, everything from
collectable old-fashioned tea sets to tea
towels and oven gloves. And then there
are the cakes themselves, all cooked on
the premises. Victoria sponges sit on cake
stands ready to be served by the slice,
and bite-size fairy cakes are displayed as
iced temptations in an old wooden shop
cabinet. Sweet-toothed heaven.

110–112 Columbia Road
E2 7RG
Tel 0207 729 0538
www.treacleworld.com

OLUMBIA ROAD E2

7✳LAIRD LONDON

Need a hat? This traditional gentleman's hatter is where to buy it. Fitted out like an elegant front room, Laird is dedicated to quality, classic styles that never go out of fashion. At the back of the shop an upright piano is piled high with trilbies, deer-stalkers and raffia Stetsons. Tweed flat caps hang in rows on the wall and Baker Boy caps are laid out in an old-fashioned cabinet. And if you don't know the difference between a Baker Boy and a flat cap, this is the place to find out. A lovely, old-school experience—you might even leave with a top hat!
128 Columbia Road
E2 7RG
Tel 0207 240 4240
www.lairdlondon.co.uk

9*

Vintage Heaven

9*

8*

8*

WOODEN
SPOOL
£3.50

8 ✳ BEYOND FABRICS

If you've never been tempted to take up sewing, you will after a visit here. Acres of vintage-style fabrics and countless haberdashery bits and pieces are all crammed into this tiny treasure-chest shop. To say it's a visual feast of colour and pattern doesn't do it justice. Packets of fabric scraps are arranged in a lucky dip basket, jars of buttons sit on shelves and a bright blue brick wall offsets a display of beautiful vintage ribbons.
If you're a novice, classes in such skills as quilting and patchwork are on offer in the shop's own sewing room.
67 Columbia Road
E2 7RG
Tel 0207 729 5449
www.beyond-fabrics.com

9 ✳ VINTAGE HEAVEN

There isn't a spare corner left in this shop. Every possible surface is packed with vintage glass, china, cutlery, books, fabrics; you name it, if it's from the 1940s–1960s, chances are you'll find it here. What makes this place extra special is the owner's merchandising eye. There may be mountains of stuff, but it's carefully displayed according to colour, pattern and style. One whole shelf is devoted to glass jelly moulds and butter dishes, another to orange glassware, another to flowery teapots. And on and on it goes. It may be hard to take it all in, but it will be harder to leave without buying at least one thing. If the choice overwhelms you, head out the back to the Cake Hole café. Here, yet more vintage china is not only displayed, but used to serve your tea and cakes. A hoarder's paradise.
82 Columbia Road
E2 7QB
Tel 01277 215 968
www.vintageheaven.co.uk

11✳ JONES DAIRY

Prepare to step back in time at this deli
and café, tucked into a tiny lane off the
main Columbia Road drag. The café is
in what used to be the milking shed for
eight cows and the bones of the original
working dairy are plain to see. If you can't
get a table—it's a squeeze—you can always
buy some Colchester oysters from the
table set up outside on the cobbles. In the
shop, the fittings looks unchanged from
a hundred years ago, with a thick marble
counter and wooden shelving. Luckily, the
produce has moved with the times, with
artisan bread, farm cheeses, and jams and
honeys from local suppliers.
23 Ezra Street
E2 7RH
Tel 0207 739 5372
www.jonesdairy.co.uk

13*

12*

12 ✱ PRINTERS & STATIONERS

There's something delightfully eccentric about this wine shop and café. Squeezed into a tiny, narrow space, the wine is sold at the front, displayed under several antique chandeliers. But it's through the back where things get really interesting. Venture through another room, crammed with antique bits and pieces for sale (a clue to the owner's previous profession), and you find a one-table dining room tucked out of sight. It's like being at a dinner party at an eccentric aunt's, with the menu consisting of whatever the chef decides to do that day. More food—cheese and meat platters, washed down with a glass of wine or a Bloody Mary—is served out the front at a couple of small tables and chairs.

21a Ezra Street
E2 7RH
Tel 0207 729 9496
www.printersandstationers.co.uk

13 ✱ BRAWN

Impeccable food in a laid-back and east-London-groovy setting make Brawn a must-stop eating spot. Sit at one of the old school table and chairs and order from a menu packed with meaty treats—as the name suggests, this isn't a particularly vegetarian-friendly place. With cool art on the walls, a rough concrete floor and staff who seem more like helpful friends than paid professionals, it's the perfect place for a very long lunch.

49 Columbia Road
E2 7RG
Tel 0207 729 5692
www.brawn.co

katie thomson

This beauty parlour, with its black and white tiling, retro prints and mirrored counter tops, is a celebration of classic kitsch. The Powder Room will transport you back to the glamour of the 1950s. Treat yourself to a pampering manicure or a Blitz-style 'updo' from a beauty therapist kitted out in candy pink uniform complete with jaunty netted hat. Or how about a 'Make Him Look Twice' makeup lesson? Owner Katie Thomson started out with an at-home retro pampering service of mobile Powderpuff Girls, and now has two salons, here and in Soho. She's created a wonderful world of all things girlie and pretty, the perfect place to play dress-up. And she even serves tea and biscuits to complete the experience.

The Powder Room
136 Columbia Road E2 7RG ❀ **0207 729 1365** ❧ *www.thepowderpuffgirls.com*

'You never know where inspiration's going to come from; just keep your eyes and ears peeled'

How would you define London style?

It's original and eclectic—anything goes. I love visiting other European countries but the minute I get back I am always struck by how much more interesting London style is.

Where do you go in London to be inspired?

I live in **Bethnal Green** (see page 168) and I find inspiration in abundance across the East End. I love all the markets in London and am a regular shopper. But you never know where inspiration's going to come from; just keep your eyes and ears peeled.

Your favourite local places?

I love Wilton's Music Hall (www.wiltons. org.uk)—so many super goings-on there in beautiful surroundings. Other local faves are Bethnal Green Working Men's Club (www. workersplaytime.net), never a dull night in there. I love Columbia Road in December when we do late night shopping on Wednesdays and I buy my china for the shops (and second-hand books for me) from the lovely Margaret at **Vintage Heaven** (see page

113

107). **Broadway Market** (see page 125) is great for food, on the street and in the pubs and restaurants. In my immediate vicinity, The Nelson's Head (www.nelsonshead.com) is the best local pub.

Describe your perfect out-and-about weekend?

A hearty breakfast at **E Pellici** (see page 172). It's a wonderful café that's been in the same family for over a hundred years and is now a listed building. After that my ideal weekend would be wandering around all the glorious markets of London ... Borough, Portobello, Broadway, Brick Lane, **Alfie's** (see page 210), Spitalfields to name but a few, and of course Columbia Road.

What's in your secret shopping address book?

I do most of my shopping along Columbia Road, Redchurch Street, Cheshire Street, and Spitalfields Market on Thursdays for the antiques market. East London has it all.

Where's the best place for a weekend supper?

In the East End, Brick Lane is the place for a late bite with an array of Indian eateries and fabulous salt beef bagels from the famous Brick Lane Beigel Bake, open 24 hours a day (159 Brick Lane, E1 6SB. Tel 0207 729 0616.) For a post-theatre supper in town, I like PJ's Grill (www.pjscoventgarden.co.uk), or as a special treat J. Sheekey (www.j-sheekey.co.uk).

Best place for a drink?

A super secret cocktail bar called Lounge Bohemia in Shoreditch (www.loungebohemia.com). Very good martinis! I also like the martinis in The Soho Hotel (www.firmdale.com) and I love the V&A Reading Rooms (www.vandareadingrooms.co.uk) for drinking and book shopping all in one place.

Your favourite breakfast spot?

The Premises on Hackney Road (www.premisesstudios.com) does a superb breakfast, or if you like a good kipper (I do), **Jones Dairy** just off Columbia Road (see page 108) does a great one and is a lovely place to read the papers. But the best breakfast I ever had was the Champagne breakfast created for our wedding at **Printers & Stationers** on Ezra Street (see page 111). It's an absolutely gorgeous place—I'd like my house to look like it.

Favourite cultural London sights?

The Victoria and Albert Museum (www.vam.ac.uk)—late nights on Fridays, dinner, drinks and whatever delectable delights they have on offer to see, what a treat. St Paul's (www.stpauls.co.uk), an obvious choice I know, but I often get the bus past there and am still always overwhelmed. It is just as breathtaking inside, too. And then London pubs, so many to choose from ... The Ten Bells with its Jack the Ripper history (84 Commercial Street, E1 6LY. Tel 0207 366 1721), The Grapes in Limehouse (76 Narrow Street, E14 8BP. Tel 0207 987 4396) reputedly the oldest Thames-side pub and The Magdala (www.the-magdala.com) where Ruth Ellis, the last woman to be executed in Britain, shot her lover dead.

Top three things that every visitor to London should do?

Go to the 140-year-old Columbia Road flower market for a whiff of Victorian London. Look over London from **Primrose Hill** (see page 34) or Alexandra Palace (especially for the fireworks, www.alexandrapalace.com) and go to Highgate Cemetery (www.highgate-cemetery.org). Not just for Hammer horror fans, it's a genuinely eerie and fascinating place.

SHOP

1 E5 Bakehouse
2 Arch 389
3 Stella Blunt
4 Our Patterned Hand
5 Strut

EAT & SHOP

6 Happy Kitchen
7 Broadway Market

EAT

8 Climpson & Sons
9 Wilton Way Café
10 Violet

EAT & DRINK

11 Cat & Mutton

● Train Station

Hackney Downs

Amhurst Rd

Dalston Ln

Hackney Central

Navarino Rd

Graham Rd

9

10 Wilton Way

Richmond Rd

hackney

London Ln

1
6
2

Lansdowne Dr

Middleton Rd

✳ LONDON
FIELDS ✳

London Fiel

Albion Dr

Queensbridge Rd

3

4
8
7

11

5 Ada St

Mare St

Whiston Rd

Broadway Market

london fields

east →

A Saturday outing to Broadway Market in London Fields, Hackney, is a must. As soon as you arrive, you'll notice that it's a seriously trendy hangout—coffee-sipping bright young things spill out of cafés onto the pavement, congregate in the pubs and stroll up and down the market's food and vintage clothes stalls. If you love a bit of people watching, you've come to the right place. But it's not just the market stalls that are worth a visit. The area around the green expanse of London Fields has a wealth of independent outlets, tucked into railway arches and hidden in the surrounding residential streets. No wonder it's one of the city's hippest addresses. Come and join the fun.

6*

6*

6*

1*

HACKNEY WILD

A classic pain de campagne, a blend of locally milled organic white, wholemeal and rye flours. A versatile bread with a moist, chewy crumb, perfect fresh for sandwiches or as toast with your favourite spread, beans or a full English.

INGREDIENTS

1* E5 BAKEHOUSE

As the trains rumble overhead, locals line up in this railway arch turned artisanal bakery to buy the lovingly made sourdough bread. It's a rough and ready place—corrugated iron roof, old wooden floorboards and bags of flour piled up in the corner—but there's nothing shabby about its products. The baking is done in full view of customers at the back of the arch space, with favourites like the Hackney Wild (a classic white sourdough) and Borodinsky bread (rye sourdough with molasses), selling fast. Order a coffee, pick your loaf and add a jar of Hackney Honey made from local bees to eat it with at home. You can even sign up for a Saturday baking class if you fancy it.
***Arch 395, Mentmore Terrace
E8 3PH
Tel 07548 300 244
www.e5bakehouse.com***

6* HAPPY KITCHEN

The mood is, as you'd expect from its name, upbeat at the Happy Kitchen. It really is a feel-good place. Calling itself a 'canteen, bakery & pantry', it sits in a railway arch that has been transformed into the sort of café you want to hang out in all day. With two big communal wooden benches set with old milk bottles containing flowers, big blackboards with the daily menu and quirky art on the walls, it has a lovely laid-back feel, reinforced by the very friendly staff. Food is organic and fresh, with a menu of brunch specials and lunchtime salads. Delicious. And when you've eaten, you can try your hand at chocolate making or artisan baking, in one of the café's classes. A lovely spot.
***Arch 393, Mentmore Terrace
E8 3PH
Tel 0208 525 4994
www.happykitchen.org.uk***

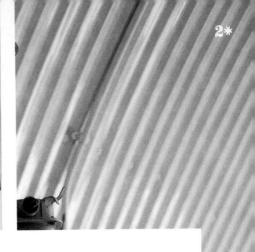

2* ARCH 389

The long, narrow space of this railway arch is crammed to the roof with retro furniture. It's a rummager's idea of heaven. From classic mid-century modern pieces to battered old trunks, antlers, mirrors and paintings, it's a mix of whatever has caught the owner's eye. Like a 1920s wooden rowing boat propped up against one wall, and an old leather pommel horse from a school gym. You're bound to find something you'll want to take home with you.

Arch 389, Mentmore Terrace
E8 3PN
Tel 07957 491 644

3* STELLA BLUNT

This tiny shop on the Broadway Marketamon strip houses a well-edited collection of chic, vintage buys. With its white-painted boards on the ceiling and sloping timber floor, the space feels more like someone's front room than a shop. But it's someone with a very good eye. In among the classic favourites like Ercol furniture and chandeliers, you'll spot quirkier items like a set of ten pin bowling skittles and a collection of old golf flagsticks. If nothing else tempts, you can leave with a greetings card made from a vintage playing card or a tin of 1960s drawing pencils.

72 Broadway Market
E8 4PH
Tel 07958 716 916

FRANKLY MY DEAR I DONT GIVE A DAMN

MORE
MODELS
DOWNSTAIRS

SKIN

3*

STRUT

UNIQUE VINTAGE AND DESIGNER FASHION BOUGHT AND SOLD

MARGIELA
WESTWOOD
COMME DES GARÇONS
ISSEY MIYAKE
BIBA
YVES SAINT LAURENT
CHLOÉ
CHANEL
THIERRY MUGLER
OSSIE CLARK
BILL GIBB
ALAÏA
YAMAMOTO
HELMUT LANG
DIOR
RAF SIMONS
COURRÈGES
PUCCI
MCQUEEN
CÉLINE

5✳STRUT

A far cry from the usual, slightly fusty, vintage clothing store, Strut is about as urban and modern-looking as it gets. With a polished concrete floor, exposed ceiling services and painted breeze block walls, everything about it says twenty-first century. The only clue to its vintage soul is the original shop fittings from Mary Quant's 1960s London store. The clothes are a mix of high-class vintage (think a full length Ossie Clark crepe dress, a Biba shirt and Gucci suitcase), hardly worn designer second hand (the likes of Stella McCartney and Martin Margiela) and a few new pieces from top end names like Balenciaga. It's a tempting mix.

2B Ada Street
E8 4QU
Tel 0207 254 8121
www.strutvintage.com

123

7✳BROADWAY MARKET

On Saturdays, Broadway Market comes
alive with stalls selling everything from
organic meat and cheese to kids' clothing
and bric-a-brac. There's even a hog
spit roast. Grab a takeaway coffee from
Climpson & Sons (see page 126) and go
for a wander. Here are a few favourites
to look out for:

Drake & Naylor: Fun, affordable
and useful vintage design from the
1950s–1980s. If your home needs an angle
poise lamp, a piece of taxidermy or set of
1970s brass swallows, you'll find it here.
www.drakeandnaylor.co.uk

Sue Goodman: Remember the Ladybird
and I-Spy books of your childhood? Sue
has stockpiled them. It will all come
flooding back as you look through the
titles. Half the fun is listening to fellow
customers gasp as they spot the book
that their eight-year-old-self loved.

Alice Gabb: There's something
quintessentially British and quirky about
turning a vintage Royal commemorative
mug into a candle. And that's what Alice
does. A 1902 King Edward VII and Queen
Alexandra Coronation mug is filled with
eco soy wax. Ditto a Queen Elizabeth II
Silver Jubilee mug. There's even Charles
and Diana wedding china ready to burn.
Lovely souvenirs for anyone after an
unusual bit of Britishness.

8✳ CLIMPSON & SONS

The spot on Broadway Market where the cool kids hang, this coffee shop is never not packed, with locals crammed into every corner and spilling out onto the pavement benches. It's all about the coffee, hand-roasted at the café's nearby roastery. It helps too, that the place looks effortlessly hip. The lovely old shop front and funky interior are a winning combination—try to find yourself a spot, if you can. For those who can't squeeze in, there's always the online coffee-selling service. Not quite the same as experiencing an espresso and a snack in person, though.

67 Broadway Market
E8 4PH
Tel 0207 812 9829
www.webcoffeeshop.co.uk

4✳ OUR PATTERNED HAND

From the window display of stacked jars filled with buttons and rolls of ribbon to the walls lined with bolts of fabric, this is a sewer's treasure trove. Vintage kimono silk and old hemp sacking sit alongside hand-blocked Liberty prints, Harris tweeds and limited edition digitally printed silks. It makes you want to grab a pattern and get dressmaking. And if you don't know one end of a needle from the other, sign up for one of the shop's sewing workshops, offering everything from 'mastering zips' to 'making an A-line skirt'.

49 Broadway Market
E8 4PH
Tel 0207 812 9912
www.ourpatternedhand.co.uk

CLIMPSON & SONS MENU

- Granola, yoghurt and fresh berries £3.50
- Bircher muesli, yoghurt pistachios & honey £3.50
- Toast with choice of spreads £1.50
- Crumpets with choice of spreads £1.80

  * Gluten free bread available.

- Chickpea & artichoke salad with grilled halloumi £5.00
- Chicken, avocado, feta and pine nuts with honey mustard dressing £5.00
- Smoked mackerel, beetroot & horseradish £5.00

- Avocado & tomato salsa on sourdough toast £2.50
  - add smoked salmon +£2.50
- Grilled halloumi & houmous sandwich £3.90
- Gourmet pies, with pea, feta & mint salad £5.50

* Ask staff for details

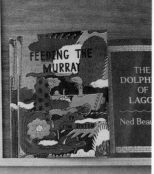

FEEDING THE MURRAY

THE
DOLPHIN
OF
LAGO

Ned Beau

LFR

London Fields Ra

la

Trance e

A New
Collection

9✳ WILTON WAY CAFÉ

How many cafés have a DJ booth
from which the local community radio
station broadcasts? This is that kind of
place, but you need to know about it to
find it. Away from the main Broadway
Market drag, it's tucked away down a
picturesque residential side street. If
only there was a café like this in every
neighbourhood. The food and coffee
are delicious, and it's a joy just to sit
here soaking up the neighbourhood
vibe. Reclaimed materials like
corrugated iron and old pieces of
wood create a laid-back feel, there's
local artists works on the walls and the
staff are smiling. Get your timing right
and visit the weekend of the Wilton
Way street fair, and you'll find the
café at the heart of it all, with a pop-up
book shop inside, vintage vans on the
street outside and even a dog show.

63 Wilton Way
E8 1BG
Tel 07793 754 776

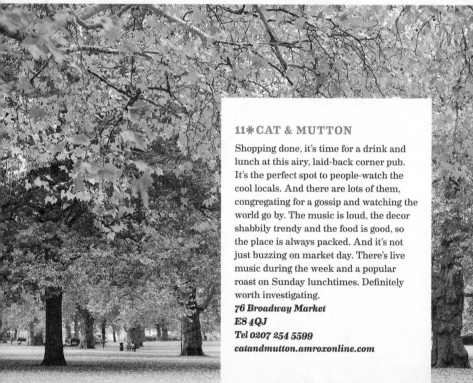

11✳CAT & MUTTON

Shopping done, it's time for a drink and lunch at this airy, laid-back corner pub. It's the perfect spot to people-watch the cool locals. And there are lots of them, congregating for a gossip and watching the world go by. The music is loud, the decor shabbily trendy and the food is good, so the place is always packed. And it's not just buzzing on market day. There's live music during the week and a popular roast on Sunday lunchtimes. Definitely worth investigating.

76 Broadway Market
E8 4QJ
Tel 0207 254 5599
catandmutton.amroxonline.com

The Cat & Mutton

Lunch 12-3

- Tomato & Basil Soup w/ Bread £5
- Pork Belly Sandwich w/ Apple Sauce & Rocket £6
- Sardines on Toast w/ Capers & Chilli Butter £8
- Deep Fried Sprats w/ Smoked Paprika Mayo & Brown Bread £6
- Pan Fried Halloumi w/ Apple, Pecan & Beetroot Dressing £7.50
- Linguine w/ Stem Broccoli, Cashel Blue Sauce & Crispy Breadcrumbs £9.50
- Homemade Burger w/ Cheddar, Dijon Chutney, Coleslaw & Chips £10
- Wild Boar & Chunky Sausages, Mash Potato, Green Beans & Gravy £9.50
- Smoked Black Pudding, Bacon, Potato & Rocket Salad w/ Poached Egg £8
- Salmon & Herring Fishcake w/ Fennel Tomato, Rocket & Tartare Sauce £10
- Devilled Lamb Kidneys w/ Bubble & Squeak £8
- Chicken Schnitzel w/ Warm Onion & Potato Salad, Cucumber & Mint Yoghurt £9.50

- Apple & Plum Crumble w/ Creme Anglaise £5
- Sticky Toffee Pudding w/ Vanilla Ice Cream £5
- Selection of Ice Cream: Cherry, Salt Caramel, Rhubarb, Vanilla, Raspberry, Banana - 2 scoops = £4 / 3 scoops = £5.50
- Selection of Neal's Yard Cheeses w/ Homemade Chutney & Oat Cakes £9.50
  (Keen's Cheddar, Cashel Blue, Stawley Goats & St. James' Soft)

131

claire ptak

It may be small, but this cake shop and café packs a punch. Violet began and still trades at Saturday's Broadway Market, but operates throughout the week at this bricks-and-mortar venue. It's a mecca for sweet-toothed aficionados who travel across London for its famous cupcakes—and a lot more besides. Owner and Hackney resident Claire Ptak worked as a pastry chef at the legendary Chez Panisse in Berkeley, California and from the moment you see the blackboard outside announcing specials like Salted Caramel Whoopie Pies, you know you're dealing with a cake creator at the top of her game. No wonder there's always a queue. Treat yourself to a slice of ginger molasses cake to take home, or sit in and enjoy the atmosphere.

VIOLET
47 Wilton Way E8 3ED ❈ 0207 275 8360 ❈ *www.violetcakes.com*

> *'I love to sit in the Rose Bakery on top of Dover Street Market overlooking the roof tops in Piccadilly'*

How would you define London style?

Coming from California where everyone has a car, I am always impressed by London women cycling and taking the Tube in awesome shoes (often heels). London girls really wear their shoes into the ground and I love that!

Where do you go in London to be inspired?

I get a lot of inspiration standing behind my stall at Broadway Market. Everyone looks amazing. I also love to sit in the Rose Bakery on top of **Dover Street Market** (see page 282) and drink tea from their lovely pots overlooking the roof tops in Piccadilly.

Your favourite local places?

I love to walk up to Dalston to eat at the Mangal Turkish Pizza (27 Stoke Newington Road, N16 8BJ. Tel 0207 254 6999) and then go see a film at the Rio Cinema (www.riocinema.org.uk). I also love the Railroad café on Morning Lane (www.railroadhackney.co.uk) run by boyfriend and girlfriend Lizzy and Matt. They cook

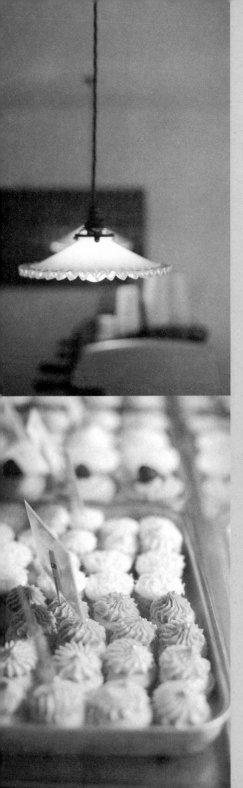

from their hearts. Of course **Towpath** (see page 143) is a favourite, too. My friends Lori and Jason started it around the same time I opened my shop. It's nice to see your friends do well in similar businesses.

What's in your secret shopping address book?

I love a little shop called Egg on Kinnerton Street (www.eggtrading.com) in West London. They have the most amazing scarves and aprons. I also love jewellery and three of my favourite designers are from London. Natasha Collis (www.natashacollis. com) for her rough cut stones and gold nuggets, Katie Hillier (www.hillierlondon. com) for her animal paperclip necklaces and Pippa Small (www.pippasmall.com) for her wonderful use of natural pearls.

Where's the best place for a weekend supper?

I am a huge fan of the River Café (www. rivercafe.co.uk). I am never disappointed and I love the room.

Best place for a drink?

I love to get a drink in the dizzying viewing gallery on the 33rd floor at Paramount (www.paramount.uk.net) in the Centre Point building on Tottenham Court Road. There is a 360-degree view of London and it reminds me where I am.

Where do you go in London to relax?

I feel very relaxed walking through the beautiful fern groves in the Epping Forest (www.eppingforestdc.gov.uk) where my husband and I take our dog Shuggie some Sundays. It is slightly outside of London but I think it still counts.

Favourite cultural London sights?

Dennis Severs' House in Spitalfields (www. dennissevershouse.co.uk). It is especially magical in the winter when it is dark so early. I also love to go to Tate Britain (www.tate.org. uk) and then take the shuttle boat to the Tate Modern. But I don't spend too long at each place. Art Gallery Overkill is a bad thing.

'I am always impressed by London women cycling and taking the Tube in awesome shoes'

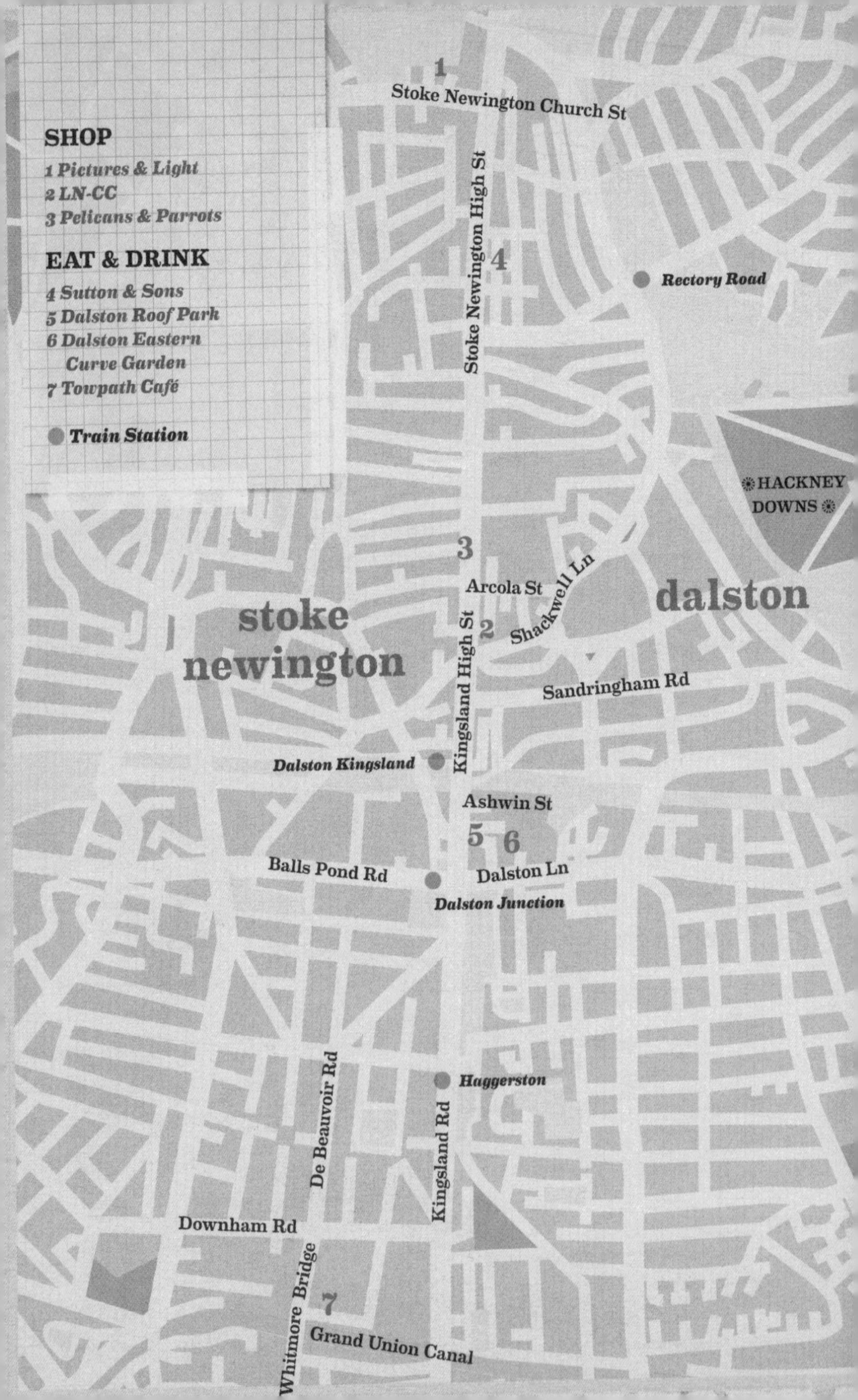

SHOP

1 *Pictures & Light*
2 *LN-CC*
3 *Pelicans & Parrots*

EAT & DRINK

4 *Sutton & Sons*
5 *Dalston Roof Park*
6 *Dalston Eastern*
  Curve Garden
7 *Towpath Café*

● *Train Station*

1

Stoke Newington Church St

Stoke Newington High St

4

● Rectory Road

❋ HACKNEY
DOWNS ❋

3

Arcola St

Shackwell Ln

stoke
newington

Kingsland High St

2

Sandringham Rd

dalston

● Dalston Kingsland

Ashwin St

5 6

Balls Pond Rd

Dalston Ln

● Dalston Junction

De Beauvoir Rd

Kingsland Rd

● Haggerston

Downham Rd

Whitmore Bridge

7

Grand Union Canal

stoke newington & dalston

east →

It's hard to imagine a better example of London as a city of contrasts. From the village-like streets of Stoke Newington, it's a short stroll to the gritty urban vibe of Dalston. They may be neighbours geographically, but the two locales couldn't be more different and the contrast is fascinating. Stroll along the leafy loveliness of Stoke Newington Church Street and then turn into Stoke Newington High Street and enter a different zone. While Stoke Newington is a pocket of slow-paced, genteel London life, Dalston is where the younger, cooler crowd are congregating. Watching the two worlds collide is what makes London such an endlessly fascinating place to be.

1✹ PICTURES & LIGHT

Owner Justine Blair has a brilliant eye for style, and her shop reflects her love of both vintage and new design. The walls are hung with a mass of vintage mirrors and the shelves lined with old pottery and coloured glassware. A cabinet shelf of delicately coloured buttons looks like a tray of sweets. Local artists' prints have pride of place alongside vintage Cuban film posters, while one-off touches of madness, like a turn-of-the-century string dispenser fashioned as a woman's head (the string comes out through her mouth), add the odd element of surprise.
41 Stoke Newington Church Street
N16 0NX
Tel 0207 923 7923

2✹ LN-CC

Possibly the winner of 'London's most hidden shop' award, the by-appointment-only Late Night Chameleon Café (to give it its full title) is a luxury fashion empire disguised as a disused basement warehouse. For a start, there's no shop sign. Come down an alleyway, ring the buzzer and only then do you realise what's been created in this former boxing gym. Quite literally, a whole new world. More like a stage set than a shop interior, you enter through a corridor of trees—the 'forest'—and then walk through another tunnel of plywood and Perspex panels. The effect is surreal. The clothes themselves, when you get to them, are high end, a mix of upcoming designers and established labels. But even if you don't buy a thing, it's worth visiting for the experience. There's also a bookshop and club space (used for private events). No wonder the likes of Coldplay and Kanye West are customers—no one would know they were here.
18 Shacklewell Lane
E8 2EZ
Tel 0203 174 0736
www.ln-cc.com

5✳

4✳

4✳ SUTTON & SONS

Forget images of a greasy local chippie. This is funky fish and chips. The decor is stripped wood communal benches, chic industrial light fittings, cool black-and-white tiling on the walls and a stylish line-drawn mural of local scenes that runs the length of the room. As for the food, how about the catch of the day, grilled British sea bass? Or grilled line-caught mackerel? The local chippie reinvented.
90 Stoke Newington High Street
N16 7NY
Tel 0207 249 6444

5✳ DALSTON ROOF PARK

Climb the sixty-plus stairs of this Victorian building (a warning: there's no lift), and you come out onto an unexpected green space. OK, it's not grass but astroturf, but with raised beds growing flowers, tomatoes, strawberries, lettuce and other assorted veg, it's not what you imagine in the heart of the East End. The rooftop bar is open seasonally (check the website for details), hosting film nights, live DJs and other local events. Even better, the whole enterprise is run as a charity, with money raised going to local community projects. But just come for the views—sipping a drink as you gaze out over the cityscape makes it well worth the climb.
The Print House
18 Ashwin Street
E8 3DL
www.bootstrapcompany.co.uk

7*

6*

6✱ DALSTON EASTERN CURVE GARDEN

This charming community garden, an oasis in the midst of an urban setting, is as gritty as it gets. Created on the site of the abandoned Eastern Curve railway line, it's cared for by local residents whose green fingers have conjured up a flower, herb and vegetable-filled paradise. Stroll along the boardwalk made from old railway sleepers and marvel at what can be grown right in the heart of the city. That's not all: a clay oven means that you can enjoy a glass of wine and slice of home-baked pizza, and there are regular live music and arts events.

13 Dalston Lane
E8 3DF
Tel 0207 503 1386
www.dalstongarden.com

7✱ TOWPATH CAFÉ

As its name suggests, this canal-side café sits right on the water's edge. With trendy apartment redevelopments in one direction and inner city housing estates in the other, this funky coffee spot is tucked into the ground floor of a warehouse block, overlooking the Regent's Canal. More a hole in the wall than a café, it boasts one tiny inside seating area and several colourful metal tables and chairs on the canal path. The open kitchen and coffee bar are set behind panels of reclaimed wood, adding to the café's laidback, casual vibe—a mood reinforced by the no-phone, no-bookings nature of the place. Just turn up, hope for a table in the sun, and enjoy the first-class coffee.

Canal Towpath
Between Whitmore Bridge and Kingsland Road Bridge
N1 5SB

juliet da silva

Along with co-owner Ochuko Ojiri, Juliet da Silva has created a quirkily chic vintage haven on this scruffy-but-cool stretch of an East London high street. With Dalston rapidly turning itself into the go-to zone for London's hip young things, it's no surprise that Pelicans & Parrots is top of the list for interiors stylists and anyone who loves a well-chosen retro buy. For the home, you'll find Victorian curiosities, old prints, antlers, glass pharmacy jars, even a stuffed peacock. And for your wardrobe there's a well-edited selection of vintage fashion finds. Juliet also throws some contemporary buys into the mix—like Abigail Ahern's kooky lamp bases (see page 30)—so that the whole effect is modern rather than dated. Expect some surprises, too. A vivid red-feathered Notting Hill carnival headdress isn't one for shrinking violets.

Pelicans & Parrots
40 Stoke Newington Road N16 7XJ ❋ 0203 215 2083 ❋ www.pelicansandparrots.com

> 'Various carnival bands put on club nights all around London'

How would you define London style?
Effortless elegance.

Where do you go in London to be inspired?
The Thursday antiques market in Spitalfields (www.oldspitalfieldmarket.com). It's great for unusual objects and colourful characters.

Your favourite local places?
Ridley Road Market has a great Trinidadian roti stall at weekends.

Describe your perfect out-and-about weekend?
People-watching in London Fields Hackney, cocktails, then on to a good Soca night for dance. Various carnival bands put on club nights all around London.

What's in your secret shopping address book?
Mawi on Calvert Avenue in Shoreditch (www.mawi.co.uk). It's a piece of West End luxury hidden in the east. Great for a window shop.

145

Where's the best place for a weekend supper?

Canteen in Spitalfields (www.canteen.co.uk). It's classic British food: local and informal.

Best place for a drink?

Bardens Boudoir next to our shop in Dalston (www.bardensboudoir.co.uk). It's so easy, down-to-earth and reasonably priced. Plus, it's right next door!

Your favourite breakfast spot?

Shoreditch House (see page 161) is a nice start to the day and the views from the rooftop are great.

Favourite cultural London sights?

I like Trellick Tower in west London and I never tire of the view as you drive over Tower Bridge.

Top three things that every visitor to London should do?

Visit Notting Hill Carnival on August bank holiday weekend, preferably in a Carnival costume. Go to a car boot sale; it's a good way to meet the real locals of any area. Princess May in Dalston is excellent (www.thelondoncarbootco.co.uk). And have a coffee in Allpress on Redchurch Street (58 Redchurch Street, E2 7DP. Tel 0207 749 1780). Delicious.

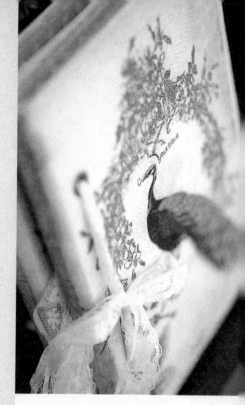

SHOP

1 *Present*
2 *Labour and Wait*
3 *Oscars Interiors*
4 *Blitz*
5 *Tatty Devine*
6 *Maison Trois Garçons*
7 *Start London*

EAT & DRINK

8 *The Book Club*
9 *The Owl & Pussycat*
10 *Pizza East*
11 *Albion*

EAT, DRINK, SLEEP (& SWIM!)

12 *Shoreditch House*

SLEEP

13 *40 Winks*

● *Tube Station*
● *Train Station*

Hoxton

bethnal green

Calvert Ave

Rivington St 7

1   11 6 2

9 Redchurch St

Great Eastern St

Tabernacle St

Paul St

Leonard St 8

Bethnal Green Rd

5

10 12   Cheshire St 3

Shoreditch High Street

shoreditch

Shoreditch High St

Brick Lane

Hanbury St 4

13

Liverpool Street

Shoreditch

If there's a hipper area in town right now, I'm struggling to think of it. Dalston may have the up-and-coming edge, but Shoreditch is still the place where the hordes of skinny-jeaned trendies flock. It's got it all. Cool, independent shops and cafés, markets, chic interiors boutiques, edgy record shops, grungy vintage emporiums and a hefty dose of gritty urban style. At the weekend, expect crowds and world-class people watching. Go for a wander, and if you can swing it, end the day on the rooftop of Shoreditch House private member's club. The best spot in town to survey the scene.

1✳PRESENT

This cult menswear store is a mecca for men who want to look fashionable but not too trend-led. Shopping starts with a coffee, made by the in-store barista—how many clothes shops offer that? It pretty much sets the tone: unexpected, hip and a bit quirky. The shop itself, with its original Golden Horn Cigarette Company frontage, is a sleek industrial-like space, complete with polished concrete floor and effortlessly cool shop assistants (all unfailingly friendly). Alongside the clothes—a perfectly curated mix of labels, with a focus on styles with heritage and a bit of a twist—are accessories, design books, magazines and the odd candle or two. And if you're really stuck, an Uzi Submachine Gun Paper Model Kit or a bottle of Aesop animal shampoo should do the trick.

140 Shoreditch High Street
E1 6JE
Tel 0207 033 0500
www.present-london.com

2*

2

3*

3

2✱ LABOUR AND WAIT

Who'd have thought that a shop that describes its stock as 'traditional products for the home' could be so stylish. Forget the dingy corner hardware store. This is an institution, famous for its meticulously presented and cleverly merchandised range of basic household wares. Classic, utilitarian and functional objects are celebrated as things of style. And so they should be. Of course, there's no plastic tat, just beautifully made wood and metal goods, but when even a container of rubber hot water bottles looks elegant, it's testament to how brilliantly put together the whole place is. You will leave with a giant ball of string you never knew you wanted—but that you will cherish.
85 Redchurch Street
E2 7DJ
Tel 0207 729 6253
www.labourandwait.co.uk

3✱ OSCARS INTERIORS

If you want a table made from an old church window or a chair fashioned from a horse's saddle, this is your place. The tiny shop, in a terrace of Georgian houses, sources unusual pieces and turns them into bespoke commissions for clients. Often on a grand sale. But that doesn't mean you can't go in and buy a candle. The charming owners will happily explain the heritage of the stock and are clearly passionate about every single item on the shop floor, down to the smallest bit of pottery. Downstairs, a gallery space showcases local artists.
18 Cheshire Street
E2 6EH
Tel 0207 739 7122
www.oscarsinteriors.com

4✳ BLITZ

If you think you're not a fan of vintage clothing, this place will change your mind. On the scale of a department store, the vast space is an old furniture factory that has been transformed into a destination in its own right. There are clothes, of course—nothing shoddy, just rails and rails of hand-picked, beautifully presented styles, most of which barely look worn—but there's also antique furniture, records and books, complete with squashy leather sofas to read them in. Oh, and a coffee bar. With its exposed brick walls, old wood floors and chandeliers hanging from the cavernous ceilings, this is vintage with polish.

55–59 Hanbury Street
E1 5JP
Tel 0207 377 0730
www.blitzlondon.co.uk

5✳ TATTY DEVINE

This cult London jewellery label is loved for its cheeky and quirky Perspex jewellery, all of it made within a short walk of the shop. A very British sense of humour shines through, like in a giant lobster necklace or an Inspector Clouseau-like moustache hanging on a chain. Their bright custom-made name necklaces are big sellers—even model Claudia Schiffer has one. Pop in. The collection is guaranteed to make you smile.

236 Brick Lane
E2 7EB
Tel 0207 739 9009
www.tattydevine.com

4

8*

9*

8*

8*

8✳ THE BOOK CLUB

Think of the coolest student common room you never had, filled with the hippest kids in the class, and that's The Book Club. An all-day, all-night venue, it's one big space of exposed brickwork, industrial lights and quirky art on the walls. Off to the side, a table tennis room is packed with bright young things engaged in a King Pong tournament. But it's not just an eating and drinking spot. As well as live music and DJs, you can pop along for an evening life drawing class, a lecture on contemporary design or a spot of speed dating. Definitely one of the local hot spots.
100 Leonard Street
EC2A 4RH
Tel 0207 684 8618
www.wearetbc.com

9✳ THE OWL & PUSSYCAT

This dark and den-like pub is a local favourite. Housed in a late-seventeenth-century Grade II listed building, it has kept all the original features (with some nineteenth-century additions) and added a cool East End twist. The low ceilings and sloping wooden floors are all intact, but look carefully at the wallpaper, and you'll see that it's actually images of tall-ships printed onto a denim-like fabric. Victorian cameo silhouette prints hang on one wall, modern art on another. The mix of historic (the pub stands on the edge of what was one of the worst nineteenth-century slums) and modern day gives the place a unique charm. Plus the fact that it's one of the best Sunday lunch spots in the area—the traditional roast is a winner. London heritage brought up to date.
34 Redchurch Street
E2 7DP
Tel 0203 487 0088
owlandpussycatshoreditch.com

10 ✳ PIZZA EAST

London's hippest pizzeria. Owned by the creators of Soho House (their Shoreditch venture is upstairs in the same vast warehouse building, see page 161), this feels more like a club than a restaurant— loud music, stripped-back industrial chic decor and lots of beautiful people. The food is, quite simply, delicious. Start with the likes of fig, burrata and honeycomb bruschetta, and then try to decide on just one choice from the pizza menu. One visit is not going to be enough.

56 Shoreditch High Street
E1 6JJ
Tel 0207 729 1888
www.pizzaeast.com

11 ✳ ALBION

This street level café and bakery, in the ground floor of the Boundary hotel, is the perfect brunch spot. A light and airy space with big doors opening onto the cobbled street, it's buzzy and crowded from 8 am to 11 pm. Specialising in traditional British fayre, breakfast is particularly good, but a late night Welsh rarebit or beef and stout pie is pretty hard to beat. As you'd expect from a place created by British design legend Sir Terence Conran, Albion is a beautifully designed room, with old wooden floors, funky industrial fittings and a mix of small and communal tables. And that Conran eye for quirky-but-cool detail is everywhere. Old tins of Lyle's Golden Syrup are used to store vintage-style cutlery, and bottles of Heinz tomato sauce and HP brown sauce have pride of place on the tables. Don't miss the shop, filled with goodies from the bakery and wooden trays of organic veg from Conran's own kitchen garden.

2–4 Boundary Street
E2 7DD
0207 729 1051
www.albioncaff.co.uk

6*

12*

6✳ MAISON TROIS GARÇONS

Trois Garçons are a local institution;
Hassan, Michel and Stefan, three
partners in work and life (or so local
legend has it), have created an empire
of a restaurant (Les Trois Garçons), bar
(LoungeLover) and now this shop. There's
even a chateau in France that can be
rented. All have the men's distinctively
camp, glamorous style stamped all over
them. This shop allows you to take a little
piece of that flamboyant aesthetic home
with you. OTT and fabulous.
45 Redchurch Street
E2 7DJ
Tel 07879 640 858
www.lestroisgarcons.com

12✳ SHOREDITCH HOUSE

Not a member of Shoreditch House, the
private members' club that's part of the
global Soho House group? Get a room ...
literally. Book yourself an overnight
stay in one of the club's gorgeously bijou
Shoreditch Rooms, and full access is
yours. Even if the club was not attached,
this would be a fantastic place to
stay. Walls are clad in pale grey wood
boarding, dark hessian matting takes the
place of carpet, and you hang your clothes
on a series of chunky hooks at picture
rail level. The rooms exude beach-hut
chic, with a casual luxe feel that you don't
often find in a city hotel. Make sure you
make full use of the club's facilities (you
can sign in a friend as well) with drinks
up on the roof garden, then dinner in the
buzzy House Kitchen restaurant. And the
best bit? An early morning swim in the
fifteen-metre rooftop pool. Always heated,
it's a perfect start to the day, whatever
time of year.
Ebor Street
E1 6AW
Tel 0207 739 5040
www.shoreditchhouse.com

13✳ 40 WINKS

You will never have slept anywhere like 40 Winks. Interior designer David Carter rents two B&B rooms (one single, one double) at the top of his 1700s Queen Anne townhouse, and the experience of entering his creatively extraordinary world is breathtaking. The house is, quite simply, magical. Every surface, every nook and cranny, has been filled with objects and art. There's too much to take in at once; you have to sit and gaze at a room for a while to appreciate all the details. The more you look, the more you notice. Crystals, lace, mirrors, velvets, shells, corals, feathers—they're all used to adorn the house. The main bedroom is styled like the boudoir of a well-travelled lady, complete with a pile of old suitcases with handwritten luggage labels and a sailor's hat. Everything has a story to tell. Book well ahead to avoid disappointment—the house is a favourite with visiting magazine teams shooting in London—and make sure you have a good look around. London's most original check-in, without a doubt.

109 Mile End Road
E1 4UJ
Tel 0207 790 0259
www.40winks.org

163

brix smith-start

Start London is where the cool girls go to shop. Is it any wonder, when you look at the CV of its owner, Brix Smith-Start? Guitarist and singer with legendary 1980s Brit band The Fall. Actress. TV presenter. Boutique owner. The woman has cool coming out of every pore. And it shows in the clothes she stocks. This is properly grown-up luxury shopping—pricey labels, beautiful setting, knowledgeable staff. Brix has a perfect eye when it comes to cherry-picking the best of the new season trends, and then displaying them irresistibly. Your credit card might not be happy, but your wardrobe will be.

Start London
42–44 Rivington Street EC2A 3BN ❋ 0207 033 3951 ❋ www.start-london.com

> '*When you stand in Hyde Park you feel like you are in the country*'

How would you define London style?
Free, quirky, creative and gracefully discreet.

Where do you go in London to be inspired?
Most definitely Hyde Park and The Serpentine Gallery (www.serpentinegallery. org) on a Sunday with my husband and my dogs. When you stand in Hyde Park you feel like you are in the country.

Your favourite local places?
So many. **Bistrotheque** (see page 171) is the epicentre of the cool fashion crowd. It's like Soho, New York in the 1980s. They have a fantastic tranny cabaret and it's always a brilliant night out with wonderful food. White Cube (www.whitecube.com), an awesome gallery with ground-breaking, mentally stimulating, food for thought. Saf (www.safrestaurant.co.uk), a great vegan restaurant, so tasty you almost can't believe it's meat free! I always feel so good after eating there. Rochelle School Canteen (www.arnoldandhenderson.com) which is a well-kept secret. Tucked away behind a gate,

it's a gem to put in your restaurant black book. And finally, The George & Dragon (2–4 Hackney Road, E2 7NS. Tel 0207 012 1100), the best gay pub in London. A total Shoreditch hangout.

Best place for a drink?

The rooftop garden at **Shoreditch House** (see page 161), where my beverage of choice is an espresso martini ... but only one!

Where do you go in London to relax?

The Cowshed spa at Shoreditch House for luxury treatments. I also love The Sanctuary (www.thesanctuary.co.uk).

Favourite cultural London sights?

Tate Modern (www.tate.org.uk), the V&A (www.vam.ac.uk), the Serpentine Gallery in the summer time, **Columbia Road** (see page 94), Covent Garden flower market (www.newcoventgardenmarket.com) in the mornings and The Globe Theatre (www.shakespearesglobe.com).

Describe your perfect out-and-about weekend?

I get out of the city! I go to the beach, to Camber Sands in East Sussex, with my dogs and my husband. Nestled among the sand dunes, we watch the clouds pass.

And what about a weekend in London?

I always work on Saturday so the only day off I really have is Sunday and, creatures of habit, we spend it the same way every single week. We wake up early with the dogs and have breakfast at Jamie Oliver's Fifteen (www.fifteen.net). We then drive with the dogs to Hyde Park or Kensington Gardens and do a long family walk all the way around the park. We then drive to Marylebone High Street and visit the Farmer's Market to get fruit, veg and goodies for the week to come. We also usually visit **Daunt Books** (see page 217) and each buy a book for the week. We get back in the car and drive to Whole Foods in Camden (www.wholefoodsmarket.com), do the rest of our weekly shopping and head home to spend the rest of the afternoon reading, watching TV and cuddling our dogs.

Your favourite breakfast spot?

The Rivington Grill (www.rivingtongrill.co.uk) is like our local café. Even though it's owned by Caprice Holdings and has a glamorous clientele (the crème de la crème of Brit art stars, for example), there's something relaxed and unpretentious about it and the food is utterly delicious in a classically British way.

Top three things that every visitor to London should do?

Apparently Madame Tussauds—the line never ends! Seriously though, Tate Modern (www.tate.org.uk), and take in a play in the West End. And I love the Tower of London (www.hrp.org.uk/TowerOfLondon) for its history and fantasy.

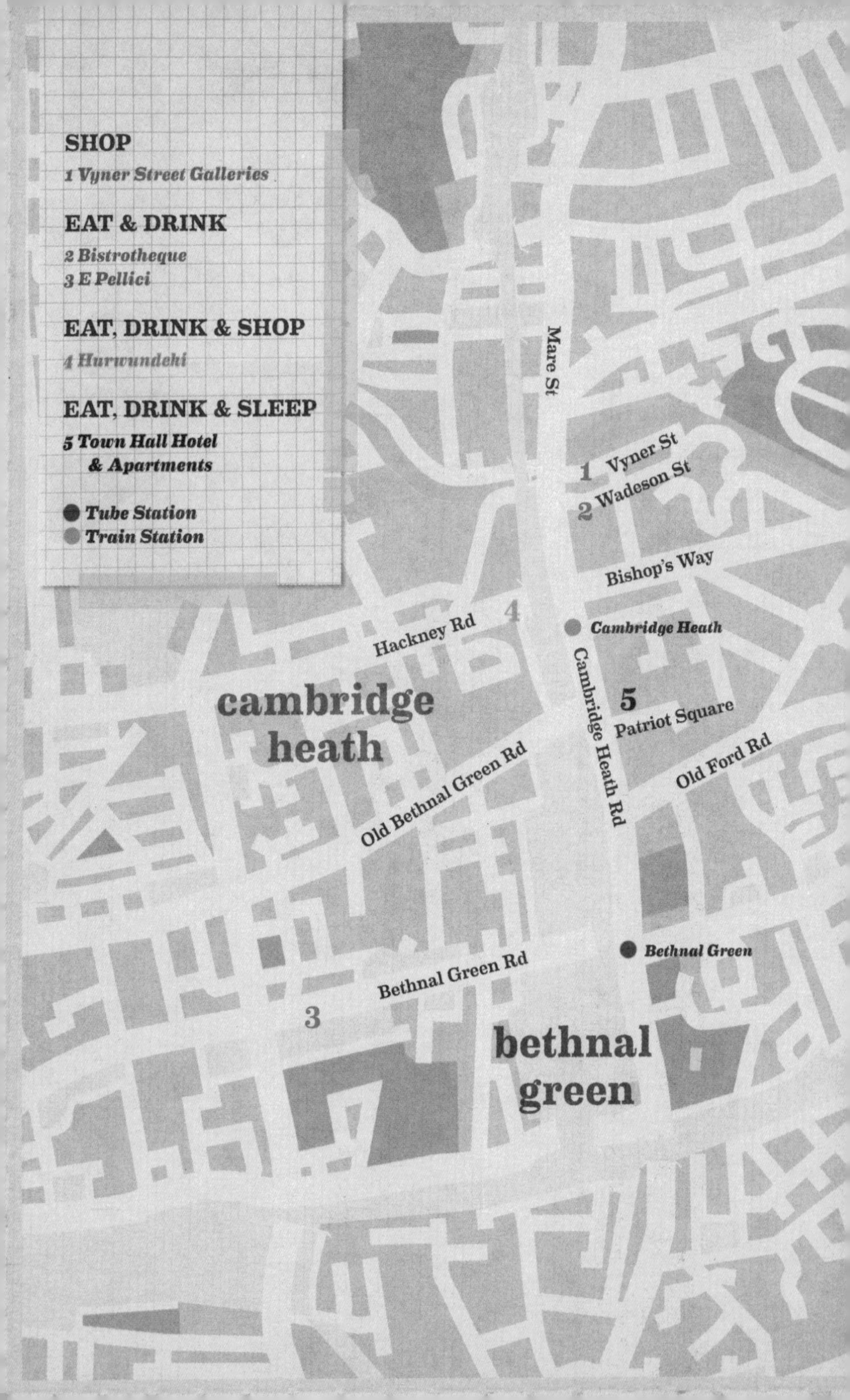

SHOP

1 Vyner Street Galleries

EAT & DRINK

2 Bistrotheque
3 E Pellici

EAT, DRINK & SHOP

4 Hurwundeki

EAT, DRINK & SLEEP

5 Town Hall Hotel
  & Apartments

● *Tube Station*
● *Train Station*

Mare St

1 Vyner St
2 Wadeson St

Bishop's Way

4

● *Cambridge Heath*

Hackney Rd

cambridge heath

Cambridge Heath Rd

5
Patriot Square

Old Bethnal Green Rd

Old Ford Rd

● *Bethnal Green*

Bethnal Green Rd

3

bethnal green

bethnal green

In the heart of London's East End, Bethnal Green is a melting pot. With a history of French Huguenot, Jewish and Bangladeshi influences, it represents everything that is so special about the city's multicultural DNA. Add to that the more recent influence of the contemporary art scene and the hub of young artists living and working in the area, and you have an intriguing mix. Rough and ready around the edges, it's worth a visit just to have a drink in the splendour of the restored Town Hall hotel. Neighbouring Shoreditch is a short stroll, and the centre of London a quick Tube ride, making this a very well-connected spot.

2✷BISTROTHEQUE

In 2004 this was one of the first
flowerings in what was then a grotty,
industrial wasteland; certainly not a
first-on-your-list area for a cool night out.
But the owners were ahead of their time
and eight years on, Bistrotheque is an
institution. The street still isn't pretty and
the neighbouring buildings still look like
shabby warehouses but people no longer
wonder if there really is a restaurant
in surrounds like these. Perennially
packed, Bistrotheque is loved by locals
and visitors alike. The restaurant occupies
an airy white space, little changed since
the building's industrial days, save for
white tiling on the walls and a chandelier.
The rough concrete floors and exposed
steel girders keep the feel gritty. Always
busy for weekend brunch (with a pianist
accompaniment), there are also plans
for an extended bar, while the cabaret
space downstairs offers colourful drag
show entertainment.
23–27 Wadeson Street
E2 9DR
Tel 0208 983 7900
www.bistrotheque.com

3✻ E PELLICI

For a sense of what turn-of-the-century Bethnal Green was like, stop off at this tiny, crowded café. There's a reason why this squeezy, wood-panelled, low-ceiling space has been granted a Grade II listing. Opened in 1900, it has remained pretty much unchanged, a gem of Art Deco style that has been run by the same family from the start. Marquetry panelling on the inside and Victorian Vitrolite glass frontage on the outside, it's a little piece of history in among the internet cafés and kebab shops on this strip of road. And the Italian food's not bad either.

332 Bethnal Green Road
E2 0AG
Tel 0207 739 4873

4✻ HURWUNDEKI

A quirky mix of café and antiques shop, this is the place to come if you want to buy an old school table along with your flat white coffee. Vintage chandeliers hang from the exposed-brick railway arches, with old paintings, stag heads and box-framed taxidermy on the walls. All of it is for sale, alongside the usual café fare of salads and sandwiches. Unusual, but it works.

299 Railway Arches
Cambridge Heath Road
E2 9HA
Tel 0207 749 0638

173

5 ✳ TOWN HALL HOTEL & APARTMENTS

This disused Edwardian town hall was brought back to life in 2011 and is now one of London's most striking hotels. The Grade II listed building has been beautifully restored and updated to create a sleek, modern place to stay that combines all the grand elements of its heritage with decidedly twenty-first-century touches. From the neoclassical frontage to the inlaid marbling and sweeping staircase in the reception, there's a sense of history wherever you look. But this is no stuffy stuck-in-a-time-warp establishment; far from it. The work of local East End artists is championed throughout the building, thanks to an open commission scheme that invited them to create site-specific work. Keep an eye out for Debbie Lawson's *Persian Moose* sculpture, fashioned from antique carpets. Not what the Edwardians would have been used to. Generously proportioned bedrooms feature lovely original parquet floors, high ceilings and lots of daylight. To be totally wowed, sneak a peak at the De Montfort Suite, a huge warehouse-sized space in the former Council Chamber, complete with a dining table for twenty and a glass-panelled staircase leading up to the sleeping area. Chef Nuno Mendes has created a destination restaurant with Viajante (and scored a Michelin star), while the more casual Corner Room is perfect for a relaxed lunch. If you're in the area, make sure you pop in.

Patriot Square
E2 9NF
Tel 0207 871 0460
www.townhallhotel.com

'Generously proportioned bedrooms feature lovely original parquet floors, high ceilings and lots of daylight'

175

danielle horn

The last thing you expect to find down the nondescript-looking Vyner Street, is a cluster of cool, contemporary art galleries. Don't be deceived by appearances. It may look like a road of warehouses, but ring on the doorbells and you'll find yourself in some of London's edgiest art spaces. Wilkinson (50–58 Vyner Street, E2 9DQ, Tel 0208 980 2662, www.wilkinsongallery. com) is the sleekest of the lot, all polished concrete floors and cavernous white exhibition spaces. But make sure to pop into Nettie Horn (25B Vyner Street, E2 9DG, Tel 0208 980 1568, www.nettiehorn.com). Owner Danielle Horn is a BBC picture publicity officer turned curator, and opened her gallery in 2007. Focusing on emerging artists from Europe and further afield, the space hosts eight shows a year.

Nettie Horn Gallery
25B Vyner Street E2 9DG ✽ 0209 980 1568 ✽ www.nettiehorn.com

'I love the views from any of the Thames bridges'

How would you define London style?
Cosmopolitan, dynamic and edgy.

Where do you go in London to be inspired?
Tate Modern (www.tate.org.uk) for a repertoire of art history in an awesome space which is an inspiration in itself; the British Museum (www.britishmuseum.org) for a journey into the past; and the British Library (www.bl.uk) for the cultural and historical source of knowledge with the beauty of viewing old authentic books.

Your favourite local places?
Broadway Market (see page 125) for the village atmosphere, authentic east London shops filled with little treasures and popular small restaurants serving hearty food from around the world; and Passing Clouds (www.passingclouds.org), a small venue in Dalston which organises fun-filled, unpretentious evenings of intimate concerts, film screenings and talks.

Where's the best place for a weekend supper?

Bistrotheque (see page 171) round the corner from Vyner Street—a very friendly and quaint place to enjoy an evening meal.

Best place for a drink?

Shoreditch House (see page 161) for a relaxing drink and a late-night swim in their rooftop swimming pool.

Your favourite breakfast spot?

Albion (see page 159) on Boundary Street does a very tasty English breakfast.

Where do you go in London to relax?

I like to relax at home followed by a walk along the Thames starting off at St Katharine Docks.

Favourite cultural London sights?

Tower Bridge, the Globe theatre (www.shakespearesglobe.com) and the views from any of the Thames bridges.

Top three things that every visitor to London should do?

Go shopping at Brick Lane and Spitalfields at weekends, with some time to relax in the numerous trendy cafés in the area. Take a walk through Hyde Park and visit the Serpentine Gallery (www.serpentinegallery.org), and discover old London through the back streets of Southwark; Borough Market and Bermondsey Street (see page 50) are a must-see, without forgetting to visit the new White Cube (www.whitecube.com) space on Bermondsey Street.

NETTIE
HORN
GALLERY

NEXUS
0800
956
2620

179

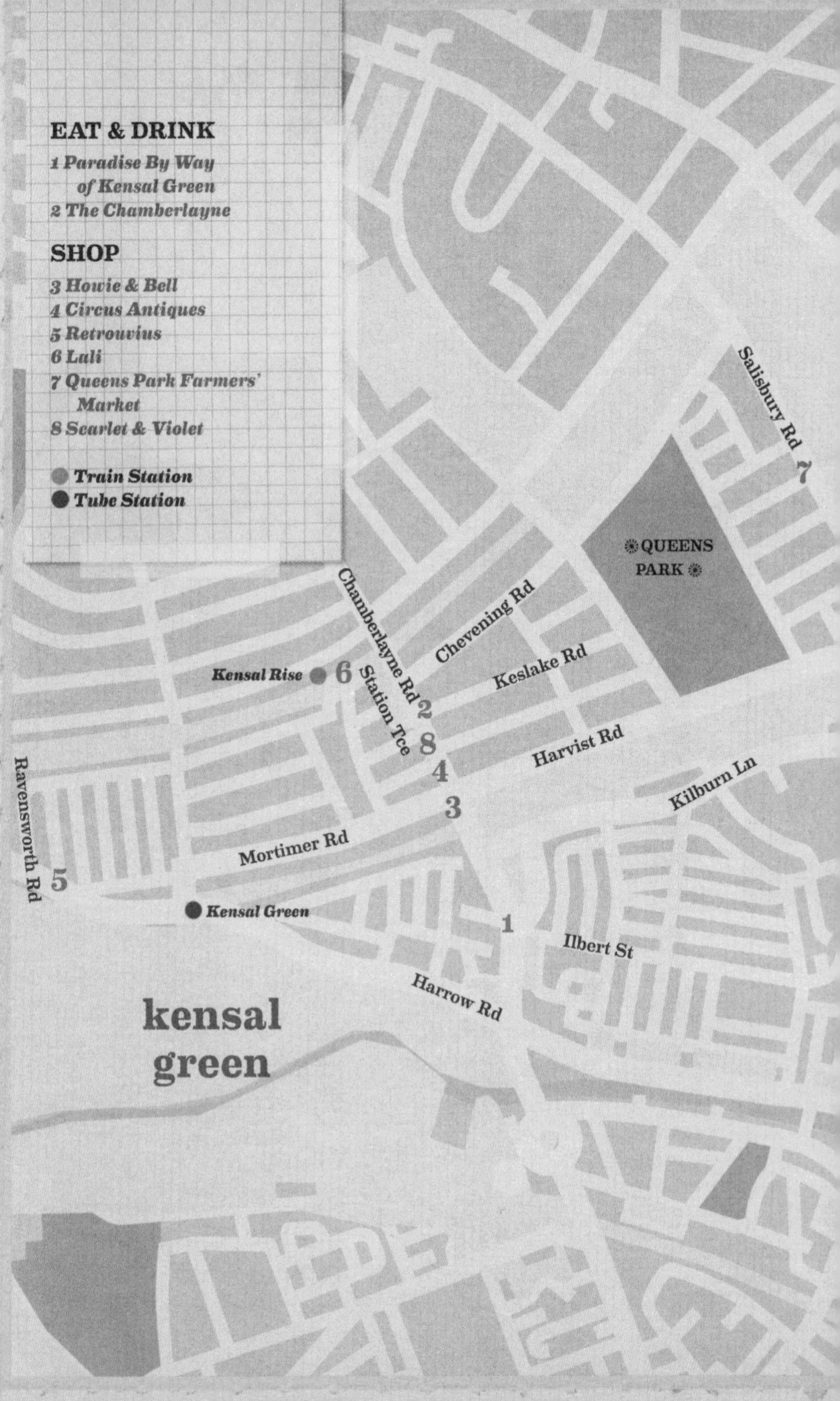

EAT & DRINK

1 Paradise By Way
   of Kensal Green
2 The Chamberlayne

SHOP

3 Howie & Bell
4 Circus Antiques
5 Retrouvius
6 Lali
7 Queens Park Farmers'
   Market
8 Scarlet & Violet

● Train Station
● Tube Station

Salisbury Rd 7

⊛ QUEENS
PARK ⊛

Chevening Rd

Chamberlayne Rd

Kensal Rise ● 6

Station Tce

Keslake Rd

8

4

Harvist Rd

3

Kilburn Ln

Ravensworth Rd

Mortimer Rd

5

● Kensal Green

1

Ilbert St

kensal
green

Harrow Rd

W

kensal rise

west

This residential pocket of northwest London has reinvented itself as a hub of cool vintage furniture shops and funky local pubs, thanks partly to its proximity to the hallowed grounds of Notting Hill and Ladbroke Grove. As house prices in those areas soared, house-hunters travelled north, transforming Kensal Rise into an unexpectedly desirable spot. A sprinkling of celebrity locals like Jade Jagger and Daniel Craig (the actor was a Kensal Riser for a while) has also helped; the chance of a bit of star-spotting in the local pub makes it well worth a visit.

1✳ PARADISE BY WAY OF KENSAL GREEN

Far more than just a humble local pub, this ornately decorated Victorian drinking establishment has hosted local supermodel Sophie Dahl's birthday celebrations and seen Jade Jagger take to the decks as DJ. With two bars and a restaurant downstairs, and three more bars and private dining spaces upstairs, it acts as a bar, restaurant, comedy venue and night club all in one. It's even launched life-drawing classes featuring burlesque dancers as models. The decor is ornately shabby chic, with chandeliers, candelabras, squashy sofas and decorative wallpaper. Book in advance for the main restaurant— the menu's impressive—or just spend a night in the bar sipping espresso martinis. Also worth checking out is the once-a-month Rag & Bow vintage sale, held on a Saturday.

19 Kilburn Lane
NW10 4AE
Tel 0208 969 0098
www.theparadise.co.uk

2✱ THE CHAMBERLAYNE

Pubs like this are what London excels at: easygoing atmosphere, just-stylish-enough decor and simple, delicious food. You'll find locals of all ages here, from the old-timers nursing pints at the bar to a younger crowd in search of drinks and dinner. Add a few children into the mix and you've got the perfect neighbourhood hang-out. Up until a few years ago, this was just another dingy pub, but a sleek makeover gave it stripped-wood floors and cool industrial-style furnishings, and it's been packed ever since. Food-wise, it's all about the meat, with huge pride taken in offering the finest British beef, sourced daily from Smithfield meat market. The steaks are some of the best you'll taste on a pub menu. The organic roast chicken is pretty good, too.
83 Chamberlayne Rd
NW10 3ND
Tel 0208 960 4311
www.thechamberlayne.com

3✱ HOWIE & BELLE

Vintage furniture lovers shouldn't miss this small stretch of Chamberlayne Road. At Howie & Belle you'll find a gorgeously decorative selection of antique furniture and curiosities, from French 1930s mirrored side tables and elegantly upholstered sofas to old wooden letters and quirky pieces of taxidermy. It's a smartly edited treasure trove that's well worth a visit.
52 Chamberlayne Road
NW10 3JH
Tel 0208 964 4553
www.howieandbelle.com

3*

6*

5*

4*

A.E. CREMER
PARIS

4*

4 ✳ CIRCUS ANTIQUES

Slightly grander than neighbouring
Howie & Belle, Circus Antiques has a chic
selection of beautifully restored vintage
furniture. Don't expect to uncover any
quirky bargains here, but if you're in the
market for 1950s French chandeliers, Art
Deco mirrored dressing tables, or even
a 1940s oak haberdashery shop counter,
this is the place to come.
60 Chamberlayne Road
NW10 3JH
Tel 0208 968 8244
www.circusantiques.co.uk

5 ✳ RETROUVIUS

This architectural salvage and design
business is one of the best known in
London, with a warehouse crammed
full of treasures rescued from building
demolitions, house clearances and
sales. Metal factory light fittings, timber
chairs from a synagogue, a pair of rabbit
skeletons—the mix is unlike anything
anywhere else. Looking for a row of
four fold-up cinema seats? You'll
find them here.
2A Ravensworth Road
NW10 5NR
Tel 0208 960 6060
www.retrouvius.com

6 ✳ LALI

This tiny shop stocks a mix of new
and vintage clothes and accessories, all
crammed into a space so small that if you
blink you'll miss it. It's worth seeking out
though. Golden oldies include labels like
Chanel, Valentino and Balenciaga, while
there are new buys from the owner's own
Bi La Li label, among others.
15 Station Terrace
NW10 5RX
Tel 0208 968 9130

7 ✷ QUEENS PARK FARMERS' MARKET

This Sunday morning food market has a reputation as one of the starriest in London. It's not strictly in Kensal Rise, but it's a short walk across Queens Park, and you might catch film star Thandie Newton and her family queuing for the fish man. With stalls selling deliciously fresh produce plus breads, cheeses and cakes, it's no wonder it's packed every week. The barbecue 'sausage in a bun' stall is particularly popular.

Sunday 10 am–2 pm
Salusbury Primary School
Salusbury Road
NW6 6RG
www.lfm.org.uk/markets/queens-park

189

victoria brotherson

To call Scarlet & Violet a small local florist is to wildly underestimate it. This crammed-to-bursting space is one of the most influential and stylish flower shops in London. Owned by Kensal Rise resident Victoria Brotherson, its just-picked-from-the-garden seasonal bouquets are regularly sent by the likes of Nigella Lawson and every magazine editor in town, and it's the first choice for fashionable clients like Hermès and Louis Vuitton who use Victoria to decorate their events. For locals, it's a lovely spot to linger while choosing a couple of bunches of blooms. The Christmas wreaths are legendary.

SCARLET & VIOLET
76 Chamberlayne Road NW 10 3JJ ❀ **0208 969 9446** ❀ *www.scarletandviolet.com*

'I love looking at front door colours, window boxes and peeping through the occasional open shutter'

How would you define London style?

I think London is driven creatively by pockets of people all spurring each other on to push the boundaries of their profession. It's not so much about toeing the style lines of elegance and taste, it's more risky and often much more homemade and independent than that.

Where do you go in London to be inspired?

As part of my job I go to private homes— these are a real display of London's aesthetic. Even just from the outside, I love looking at front door colours, window boxes and peeping through the occasional open shutter.

Your favourite local places?

Portobello and **Golborne Roads** (see page 194) on Fridays and Sundays. They're a hoarder's paradise. Have a little cash in your pocket or you'll miss the most perfect item you've ever seen and it could be a macramé basket, a stash of buttons or an amazing pair of giant urns.

191

Describe your perfect out-and-about weekend?

A dog walk on Hampstead Heath or Hyde Park and then a sausage roll at **Queens Park Farmers' Market** (see page 188).

What's in your secret shopping address book?

Retrouvius (see page 187), **Circus Antiques** (see page 187), **Howie & Belle** (see page 184) and **Alfies Antique Market** (see page 210). All are a stone's throw from me so if I need a quick shot of inspiration—or a chair for a client to sit on in the office—they are my first port of call. Each is different. Retrouvius has ever-changing, completely amazing but generally large pieces, Howie & Belle has beautifully perfect and weirdly accessible smalls from chairs to butterflies to lamps and Alfies is always brilliant inspiration.

Best place for a drink?

The Chamberlayne (see page 184), about 400 yards from my front door, for a delicious steak or half chicken and chips with a Bloody Mary.

Your favourite breakfast spot?

Toms on Westbourne Grove (www.tomsdeli.co.uk) is an old favourite for sausage sandwiches and eggs Benedict and a cappuccino.

Where do you go in London to relax?

Richmond Park (www.royalparks.gov.uk/Richmond-Park.aspx) is the perfect place to go to switch off. Once inside the boundary roads you are kind of transported to Narnia. Even with the families of cyclists it is an amazing place that always has quiet and peaceful pockets.

Favourite cultural London sights?

The Summer Exhibition at the Royal Academy (www.royalacademy.org.uk) makes me feel alive and refreshed. The Turbine Hall at Tate Modern (www.tate.org.uk) for the space and the calm and The Wallace Collection (www.wallacecollection.org)—if I go alone I transport myself back to a time without any responsibility and just gaze and enjoy a wander.

Top three things that every visitor to London should do?

Have afternoon tea at Claridge's (www.claridges.co.uk), get on an open-top bus and see all the amazing architecture we have and walk up **Columbia Road** early on a Sunday morning (see page 94).

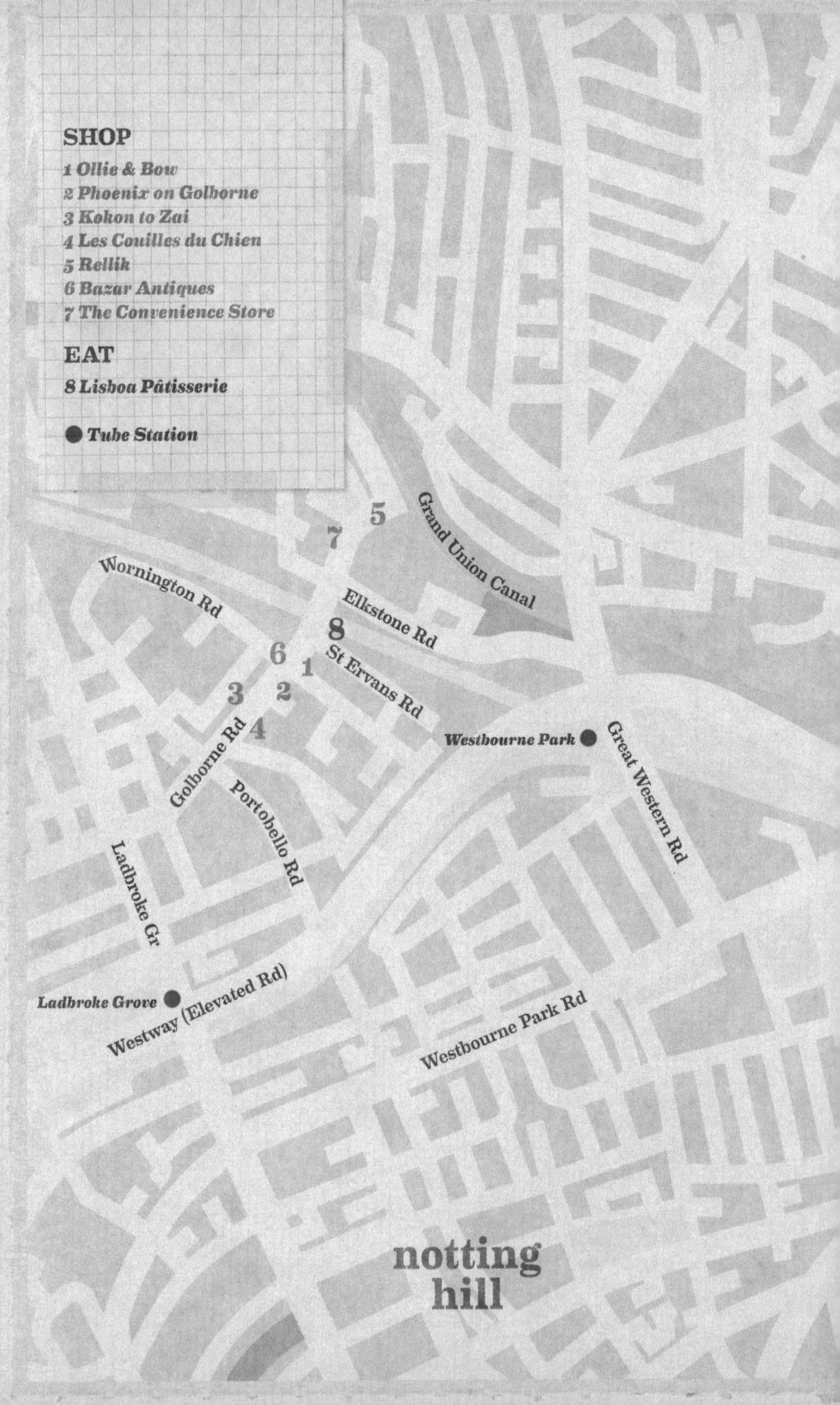

SHOP

1 Ollie & Bow
2 Phoenix on Golborne
3 Kokon to Zai
4 Les Couilles du Chien
5 Rellik
6 Bazar Antiques
7 The Convenience Store

EAT

8 Lisboa Pâtisserie

● Tube Station

Grand Union Canal

5

7

Wornington Rd

Elkstone Rd

8

6 1

St Ervans Rd

3   2

Golborne Rd

4

Westbourne Park ●

Great Western Rd

Portobello Rd

Ladbroke Gr

Ladbroke Grove ●

Westway (Elevated Rd)

Westbourne Park Rd

notting
hill

notting hill

west

Londoners tend to avoid Portobello Market—too full of tourists buying overpriced antiques and trying to find the bookshop run by Hugh Grant in Notting Hill. Little do the visiting crowds realise that they're missing the area's real treasure, Golborne Road. At the north end of Portobello Road, further than most tourists ever venture, this short street is where you'll find those in the know on a Friday and Saturday, browsing the kerbside bric-a-brac stalls and hunting for interiors treasures at the various antique furniture shops. It is very much Notting Hill for locals, so do yourself a favour and join them. One tip: a lot of the shops are open at weekends only, so check with them before you visit.

2*

2*

1*

2*

1✳ OLLIE & BOW

If this place were any more crammed, you wouldn't be able to get through the door. A mix of deco, retro and random shabby chic items, it's an irresistible spot to rummage and hunt down something unique for your home. Some pieces are obviously stylish—a 1930s oak-and-glass-fronted haberdasher's cupboard—while others are quirkily eccentric; dentist's chair, anyone? Make sure you venture down to the basement back room. Dimly lit and piled high with what looks like junk, it might just be where you uncover some treasure.

69 Golborne Road
W10 5NP
Tel 07768 790 725

2✳ PHOENIX ON GOLBORNE

Owner Jess Gilderstone has assembled a gorgeously edited selection of vintage and antique homewares, the majority of it dating from 1900–1920. Her aim is to mix useful bits of furniture like dining tables and dressers with cheaper, quirkier items such as painted watering cans, vases and bread bins. All of it is displayed to perfection, thanks to Jess's bang-on eye for styling. If you visit, be sure to say hello to the shop's resident cockapoos Bella and Molly, Jess's adorable cocker spaniel/poodle mix dogs.

67 Golborne Road
W10 5NP
Tel 0208 694 8123
www.phoenixongolborne.co.uk

3✳ KOKON TO ZAI

This beautiful old butcher's shop is a Victorian treasure. With its tiled frontage and mosaic entrance, it's a unique shopping experience from the second you cross the threshold. Inside, the eclectic mood continues. Thistle-design tiles, a solid marble counter top and a delicately mosaic-tiled floor all make it worth a visit for the interior alone. The merchandise will intrigue you. A mix of fashion and lifestyle items, the overall mood is *Alice In Wonderland* meets *Pirates of the Caribbean*, with skull motives, stag beatles, feathers, candles and butterflies. No wonder the likes of Kate Moss and Jade Jagger are fans. Both have bought artwork of a stage set fashioned from cut-up pieces of the *London Illustrated Post* newspaper. Stunning.

86 Golborne Road
W10 5PS
Tel 0208 960 3736

4✳ LES COUILLES DU CHIEN

Another piled-high treasure trove, but with slightly more space to view items than some of its Golborne Road neighbours. It's no wonder that sixty per cent of the business is done with other dealers; owner Jerome Dodd has been here for twenty-one years and he has an impeccable eye for a good buy (and a good sense of humour when it comes to shop names). From beautifully chosen pieces of furniture to exquisite chandeliers and mirrors, and smaller items like pieces of coral and butterflies displayed under Victorian domes, the shop is a delight. Even the stuffed badger that greets you on arrival manages to look stylish.

65 Golborne Road
W10 5NP
Tel 0208 968 0099
www.lescouillesduchien.co.uk

5✳ RELLIK

The mothership of seriously collectible vintage, Rellik is where aficionados come for pieces by some of the greatest names in fashion history. Ossie Clark, Yves Saint Laurent, Chanel, Pucci, Christian Dior ... You'll find them all on the crammed rails of this tiny shop, plus an enticing selection of accessories, from affordable costume jewellery to pricier designs. Don't be put off by the location—on a scruffy corner surrounded by less than salubrious high-rise housing—this is *the* spot for a vintage buy that you'll treasure.

8 Golborne Road
W10 5NW
Tel 0208 962 0089
www.relliklondon.co.uk

201

6✳BAZAR ANTIQUES

A contrast to the theatricality of many
of the other shops on the strip, this
is a pocket of chic French charm.
Specialising in homeware from
France from around 1850–1950, it's got
everything from beautiful iron garden
furniture and a set of old science lab
chairs to larger armoires and dressers.
There are also plenty of cheaper pieces
of glass and crockery. A lovely, tranquil
shopping experience.
82 Golborne Road
W10 5PS
Tel 0208 969 6262

8✳LISBOA PÂTISSERIE

Not glam, not stylish, but the purveyors
of the most delicious Portuguese custard
tarts in London. Do not leave Golborne
Road without stopping off for one.
57 Golborne Road
W10 5NR
Tel 0208 968 5242

6*

andrew ibi

At the scruffy Trellick Tower end of Golborne Road (the 1960s concrete block of flats that dominates this part of west London), you'll find one of the most forward-looking fashion stores in town. The unlikely setting is a far cry from the chi chi fashionista haunts elsewhere in the city, but that hasn't stopped Andrew Ibi opening The Convenience Store, specialising in some of style's most avant-garde labels. A designer himself, Andrew's shop is a temple of cutting-edge fashion talent, with the clothes hung like art exhibits on delicate metal threads. No surprise that he also uses his shop for exhibitions and cultural events, and prides himself on doing things slightly differently. Don't expect easy-to-wear, fast fashion. But do expect clothes that will intrigue and challenge you.

THE CONVENIENCE STORE
1a Hazlewood Tower, Golborne Gardens W10 5DT ✽ 0208 968 9095 ✽
www.theconveniencestorefashion.co.uk

'London's complex community culture is my inspiration'

How would you define London style?

London is a place of cultural exchange and freedom of expression. Its style has been evolving since the 1950s and is still heavily influenced and driven by counter-cultural groups and youth sub-cultures. It's hard to pinpoint as a definitive look but in essence it's progressive, informed, creative, expressive and diverse.

Where do you go in London to be inspired?

As a designer there are many traditional points of reference. There are galleries and museums in abundance, but I prefer London's complex community culture. There are authentic pockets all around us. I'm lucky enough to have a panoramic view of W10 and the inspiration is cross-cultural. Local is my true inspiration.

Your favourite local places?

Golborne Road really is an amazing street and plays host to many of my daily routines. The Dock Kitchen (www.dockkitchen. co.uk) is amazing for a casual but formal lunch. Trini Flava, a local food stall on Golborne Road run by Sheldon and Tina, is the place I frequent most for an authentic chicken curry. **Rellik** (see page 200), my neighbouring shop, is a very inspiring place for me. I have to mention Pizza East Portobello (www. pizzaeast.com) as well—a welcome addition to the street, informal and convenient. The other side of the world, Kingsland Road in Hackney, has its own brightly shining stars—I love the Mangal Ocakbasi (www.mangal1.com) Turkish restaurant; very local and exceptional quality.

Describe your perfect out-and-about weekend?

Saturday is really about the store but Sunday is a family day and will usually involve a mini escape, some relaxation, good food and nothing too exhilarating or exhausting. I now consider time, space and the ability to relax as a true luxury. I like lunch at **The Wapping Project** (see page 286) with a good bottle of wine and then off to The Diana Memorial Playground in Kensington Gardens. My son loves the pirate ship!

What's in your secret shopping address book?

I don't shop so much in London these days but Layers on Conduit Street (www.layerslondon.com) provides a low key and artisanal aesthetic, suitable to my clothing style. Honest Jon's records on Portobello Road (www.honestjons. com) is still a place I shop for vinyl as is Sounds of The Universe in Soho (www. soundsoftheuniverse.com).

Where's the best place for a weekend supper?

The Wapping Project, I'm really glad I found it; it's just a really clever and interesting place complemented by some great food and wine. However, I was taken to Dinner at Heston Blumenthal's restaurant (www. dinnerbyheston.com) for my birthday and I must admit it was sublime.

Best place for a drink?

The Metropolitan Pub (www. themetropolitanw11.co.uk); it's my local. I've given up on bars that are too cool and too expensive.

Favourite cultural London sights?

The V&A museum has incredibly well curated exhibitions. If you want something a little more obscure, try The Museum of Everything (www. museumofeverything.com) or Sir John Soane's Museum (www.soane.org).

Top three things that every visitor to London should do?

Steer clear of Oxford Street and check out east London. Personally I'm a 'west is best' guy, but I can't deny the energy and creativity of the East End. Redchurch Street is the new hot location but still visit Hoxton and Brick Lane. Locate authentic local London— Dalston, Brixton or Golborne Road will suffice—and please sample the local food. Finally, visit St Paul's Cathedral (www.stpauls.co.uk) for some historical context and a sense of London's true architectural beauty.

'London is a place of
cultural exchange and
freedom of expression'

SHOP

1 Margaret Howell
2 Alfies
3 Andrew Nebbett Antiques
4 The Façade
5 Matches
6 Daunt Books
7 VV Rouleaux
8 Le Labo
9 KJs Laundry

EAT & DRINK

10 Purl
11 The Providores

EAT & SHOP

12 Comptoir Libanais
13 La Fromagerie

● Tube Station
● Train Station

REGENT'S PARK

QUEEN MARY'S GARDENS

lisson grove

Park Rd

Church St

3 2   4

Lisson Gr

Marylebone

Marylebone Rd

Seymour Pl

Edgware Road

Baker Street

Marylebone High St

Regent's Park

8 Devonshire st

Weymouth St

Paddington St

Gloucester Pl

Baker St

Blandford St 10

13 5

6

11

New Cavendish St

George St

marylebone

7

9   1

Thayer St

12

Wigmore St

Cmarylebone

The Great British High Street is an endangered species. In an era of chain stores and identikit rows of shops— same coffee chain, same fast fashion shop, same supermarket—Marylebone High Street and its surrounds is a rare thing. Packed with small, independent shops and an atmosphere all its own, it is one of London's most popular shopping parades and together with the surrounding streets, a lovely part of town for a wander.

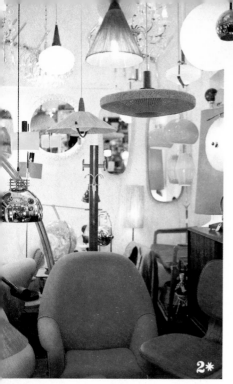

1✳ MARGARET HOWELL

This shop is the ultimate in understated British good taste. Everything about it is quietly just right. Margaret Howell is known for her beautifully crafted, elegant clothes, and the shop reflects that. Lots of natural light, white walls and old, worn floorboards—simple. There's no interior design 'concept' here. Instead, you'll find the perfect tailored shirt, the best-cut pair of trousers and a chunky cashmere knit. Oh, and maybe something vintage for the home; the designer is passionate about twentieth-century design and showcases some beautiful furniture here, alongside a few carefully chosen modern bits and pieces of homeware. Not cheap but very classy.

34 Wigmore Street
W1U 2RS
www.margarethowell.co.uk
Tel 0207 009 9009

2✳ ALFIES

Ask any fashionable London shopper where is top of their little black book of must-visits and the chances are Alfies will be on the list. More than just a shop, it's a rabbit warren of some of the city's very best dealers in antiques, vintage and twentieth-century design. It's also London's largest indoor market, covering four floors and over 35,000 square feet. The range of choice is bewildering, with literally everything covered, from a fun piece of leopard print 1950s clothing to an astonishing antique Murano glass chandelier. Big, small, affordable, out-of-this-world, it's all here. The place is a day-trip in itself. The location—a decidedly scruffy market street—may look unpromising but don't be put off. This is one of London's most exciting shopping locations. Step inside and be blown away.

13–25 Church Street
NW8 8DT
Tel 0207 723 6066
www.alfiesantiques.com

1*

211

3✳ ANDREW NEBBETT ANTIQUES

Alfies has many antique shops as neighbours, all of them worth a look. This one stands out for its clever edit of classic and quirky pieces, all in a sleek warehouse-like setting. It's quite a contrast to the higgledy-piggledy chaos of Alfies next door. Sleek leather Chesterfield sofas and elegant antique mirrors sit alongside more random finds like old glass pharmacy bottles and a late nineteenth-century mahogany hotel reception newspaper rack. And don't miss the window displays; there's always a piece of inventive styling that will maybe give you an idea or two to try at home.

35–37 Church Street
NW8 8ES
Tel 0207 723 2303
www.andrewnebbett.com

10✳ PURL

Head down some unpromising-looking stairs to the basement of this Georgian house and you'll enter one of London's most enticing bars. Channelling the spirit of a New York speakeasy, the low-ceilinged, dimly lit space is a sexy, cosy rabbit warren ... with killer cocktails. Booking is essential, especially if you want one of the booths tucked into the alcoves, each lit by its own chandelier and flickering candles. Once settled in, sit back and wait for the barman to work his magic. The house speciality is heritage cocktails served with a modern twist, so expect flourishes like liquid nitrogen steaming over the glass's rim. More mad professor's lab than swish bar. Or you might be tempted by the silver bowl on the bar top, filled to the brim with the punch of the day—complete with ladle to serve it with. With a barman this good and a venue this intoxicating, prepare to lose track of your night.

50–54 Blandford Street
W1U 7HX
Tel 0207 935 0835
www.purl-london.com

5*

5*

5*

4✳ THE FAÇADE

If you're not a chandelier fan, turn away now. This shop is like a breeding ground for them, with styles from 1910–1960 hanging from every available bit of ceiling in the cave-like space. The effect is stunning. In amongst the magical mass of crystals, you'll spot some small pieces of furniture and mirrors, but really, the chandeliers are what it's all about. Come and be blinded by the bling.
99 Lisson Grove
NW1 6UP
Tel 0207 258 2017
www.thefacade.co.uk

5✳ MATCHES

Two words: high fashion. The sleekest, most fabulous, most budget-busting names are all here. Everything a fashion mecca should be, it's small enough to feel intimate and big enough to offer the very best of every catwalk trend. And the beauty is in the details; a coffee machine and delicate china cups sit on a marble countertop and there are sofas to sink into if your credit card is feeling weary. Even the iPad-toting assistants are perfectly designed. You might wince at the prices, but come and admire it as a temple of high-end shopping.
87 Marylebone High Street
W1U 4QU
Tel 0207 487 5400
www.matchesfashion.com

4*

Ribbons　　Braids　　Trimmings

6*

6✷ DAUNT BOOKS

In this age of Amazon deals, a local bookshop is a rare sight, and Londoners treasure Daunt Books. With its dark-green-and-wood Edwardian frontage, this looks exactly how you imagine a traditional bookshop should look, and it doesn't disappoint inside. The star attraction is the long, oak gallery at the back, with a skylight running the length of the room—more university library than high street bookshop. Occasional leather armchairs encourage lingering, and the worn parquet floors add to the cosy, collegiate feel. As for the books, this was originally a travel branch, and one of the first bookshops to group books by countries—with not just guides but literature, design and general interest titles about that part of the world clustered together. Daunt also stocks general fiction and does a sterling job promoting local authors. Much more fun than browsing Amazon online.

83 Marylebone High Street
W1U 4QW
Tel 0207 224 2295
www.dauntbooks.co.uk

7✷ VV ROULEAUX

Be prepared for a wonderland of ribbons, trimmings, laces, feathers, flowers and even Christmas decorations in this crammed corner shop. No surprise that fashion and interiors stylists can't stay away—it's irresistible. You'll find reel upon reel of coloured ribbons in every texture and every width imaginable, cards wound with strings of crystal beading, pieces of lace and even huge curtain tassels in a choice of rainbow colours. You might not have a single use for a length of velvet ribbon in an exquisite shade of soft pink or blue, but you'll want some. Small beaded peacocks? Of course you want a pair of those to put on your Christmas tree. And for any Kate Middleton wannabes, the shop offers a headdress-making service, using its considerable stock of fake flowers and feathers. Just the thing for the next royal wedding.

102 Marylebone Lane
W1U 2QD
Tel 0207 224 5179
www.vvrouleaux.com

"Spray a free man and a slave with perfume
and they shall have the same smell"

Xenophon

ROSE 31

100ml 3,4 FL.OZ.

eau de parfum / vaporisateur
natural spray

Compounded: in London by Camel...
For:
SASKA GRAVILLE
...ent until: 02/10/2012

LE LABO London · 28A Devonshire Street, ...
Made in USA — 233 Elizabeth Street, New ...

LE LABO
...NEW YORK

8✳ LE LABO

This apothecary-like shop is the home
of cult perfume brand Le Labo. If
you're used to picking up a bottle of
your favourite scent in Duty Free, be
prepared for a whole new experience.
Once you've chosen your blend, it gets
hand-finished in front of you, with
a lab-coated employee blending and
mixing the final oils and then printing
a personalised label. It's quite an
operation. Shelves of medicinal bottles,
jars of dried ingredients, and a corner
glass 'lab' of Pyrex glass jars and pipettes
tell you that this is somewhere that takes
fragrance very seriously. Sit up at the
white-tiled, metal-topped counter and
watch it all unfold. Oh, and the smells
are something very special too—there's
a reason why a bottle from Le Labo is a
favourite with beauty insiders.
28a Devonshire Street
W1G 6PS
Tel 0203 441 1535
www.lelabofragrances.com

11❋ THE PROVIDORES

A contender for the best cup of coffee in London, Providores is jam-packed with locals every weekend—you'll be lucky to avoid a pavement queue. And no wonder. Brunch in the downstairs Tapa Room is something pretty special, thanks to Kiwi chef–owner Peter Gordon's unique way of combining flavours. Where else would you get poached eggs with whipped yoghurt and hot chilli butter, or Thai basil and lime waffles with tomato, sweetcorn, rocket and avocado chutney and tomato jalapeno chutney? It's not your average British brekkie. In terms of style, a giant bark Tapa cloth from Rarotonga sets the tone, with cool light fittings from NZ artist Jeremy Cole adding to the eclectic mood. Well worth a bit of a wait for a table but if you don't want to hang around, you can book brunch in the upstairs Providores space; it's more formal and less funky, but the food's still delicious.

109 Marylebone High Street
W1U 4RX
Tel 0207 935 6175
www.theprovidores.co.uk

12❋ COMPTOIR LIBANAIS

This bright and sunny café is part of a chain but it doesn't feel like it. With a quirky style and interior, it celebrates the fresh and exotic tastes of Middle Eastern cuisine. Yes, the food is delicious, but a big part of its appeal is the colourfully cheerful design. It puts you in a good mood immediately. Bright red metal chairs and tables decorated in geometric blue and turquoise shapes, metal shelves packed with enticing Middle Eastern foods, gorgeous embroidered baskets from Morocco ... It's a touch of the souk in London's West End. Pop in for a lunchtime mezze plate or for some mint tea and Lebanese sweets in the afternoon. You'll come out smiling.

65 Wigmore Street
W1U 1PZ
Tel 0207 935 1110
www.lecomptoir.co.uk

13✱LA FROMAGERIE

What began as a small cheese shop is now a food empire. Cheese is still at the heart of the business, with an on-site maturing cellar and walk-in cheese room, but there is so much more. A slice of artisan *fromage* is the minimum you'll be leaving with. There are beautifully presented seasonal fruit and vegetables, charcuterie, temptations like house-cured gravadlax, freshly baked breads and cakes, handmade ice cream ... Mouth-watering doesn't do it justice. And if you can't wait until you get home to sample the wares, the café offers tasting plates of everything. Even better, it's licensed, so you can have a cheese-and-wine lunch to try out a few lesser-known farmhouse cheeses before you buy. And how many food shops come with two disco balls hanging from the ceiling?

2–6 Moxton Street
W1U 4EW
Tel 0207 935 0341
www.lafromagerie.co.uk

kate allden
& jane ellis

Fashionistas should head straight to KJs Laundry, a perfectly edited boutique tucked down a small laneway. Owners Kate Allden and Jane Ellis have a well-honed eye for womenswear that is stylish, individual and not what you'll see everywhere else. From quirky to classic, the selection is big on lesser-known designers, as well as some of the more mainstream names. The shop itself, with its lovely worn wooden floors and pieces of vintage furniture, is as understatedly stylish as the stock it sells. Your wardrobe will thank you.

KJs Laundry
74 Marylebone Lane W1U 2PW ❖ 0207 486 7855 ❖ www.kjslaundry.com

'Londoners are very aware of style but not afraid to be themselves'

How would you define London style?

Playful and rebellious. Londoners are very aware of style but not afraid to be themselves and so the result is freedom and a lack of conformity. It's the edgiest of the fashion capitals.

Where do you go in London to be inspired?

The British Museum (www.britishmuseum. org) to dip into the cultures of the world, especially their jewellery galleries. Even though the pieces are so old they still look modern and wouldn't look out of place on today's catwalks. Very inspiring.

Your favourite local places?

The Wallace Collection (www. wallacecollection.org) for its charm—it's the perfect place to stop for tea and cake, and the rose garden at Regents Park; so many beautiful colours and varieties.

225

What's in your secret shopping address book?

Merchant Archive (www.merchantarchive.com) in Queens Park is a wonderful vintage shop. Just outside, Kempton Antique market (www.kemptonantiques.co.uk) is a bi-monthly market at Kempton racecourse which is great for finding new things for the house. Do a spot of haggling before rounding everything up into a van to drive home.

Where's the best place for a weekend supper?

Scotts (www.scotts-restaurant.com) is nice to sit at the bar, grab a quick bite and soak up the atmosphere. And the Anchor & Hope near Waterloo (36 The Cut, SE1 8LP. Tel 0207 928 9898). It's a busy gastro pub where the food is hearty and scrumptious.

Best place for a drink?

Milk and Honey (www.mlkhny.com) for the superb cocktails and quirky interior. It's like stepping into the lounge of a very rich friend with a love of the 1920s ... and it's very easy to get a bit carried away. Or The Albion in Islington (www.the-albion.co.uk) for a cosy drink—the beer garden is fab in the summer.

Your favourite breakfast spot?

Automat diner in Mayfair (www.automat-london.com) for their blueberry pancakes and Bloody Marys. It's ideally located for a stroll through Green Park or a dip into **Dover Street Market** (see page 282) afterwards.

Where do you go in London to relax?

A walk through Kew Gardens (www.kew.org) is always a tonic and it's so quintessentially British.

Favourite cultural London sights?

The view down the river from Waterloo Bridge is a great reminder of London's history and grandeur and the cobbled narrow streets around London Bridge evoke a feeling of old London with sweeping views up and down the river. Also, the London Transport Museum in Covent Garden (www.ltmuseum.co.uk) is great for kids, with lots of interactive exhibits.

Top three things that every visitor to London should do?

Have fish and chips at the Golden Hind on Marylebone Lane (73 Marylebone Lane, W1U 2PN. Tel 0207 486 3644); very popular and very yummy. Walk through Hyde Park, Green Park and St James's Park and just enjoy. And go to the top of Parliament Hill Fields or **Primrose Hill** (see page 34) to admire the views.

SHOP

1 Ben Pentreath
2 Persephone Books
3 Maggie Owen
4 The School of Life
5 Folk Clothing
6 Oliver Spencer
7 Cube
8 Darkroom

● Tube Station
● Train Station

● King's Cross
● King's Cross
   St Pancras

Euston Rd

st pancras

Gray's Inn Rd

● Euston Square

Tavistock Pl

4

Hunter St

✸CORAM'S
FIELDS✸

Bernard St

Guilford St

Millman St

6

Russell Square ●

Great Ormond St

2
7
5

Rugby St

3 1

8

Russell Sq

Lamb's Conduit St

Southampton Row

✸BRITISH
MUSEUM✸

Theobald's Rd

bloomsbury

The leafy streets and garden squares of Bloomsbury belie its very central city location. None of them more so than Lamb's Conduit Street, a cluster of independent shops that has retained its own personality, free from the curse of lookalike high street chain stores. A rarity. It's a lovely area for a wander, with cultural giant the British Museum nearby if you tire of shopping.

1✱ BEN PENTREATH

I defy you to leave this shop without
buying something for your home.
Whether it's a wooden spoon or an
antique mahogany side cabinet, there
is something to tempt every budget.
Shelves are piled high with colourful
stacks of beautiful Penguin classics and
design books. On a small chair you'll
find a stack of exquisitely illustrated
1940s books, among them *Elizabethan
Miniatures* and *Birds of the Sea*. There's
antique furniture, prints, corals and even
plaster casts of Greek sculptural reliefs.
If that's all too much, head for the utility
side of the shop, for practical necessities
like whisks, pastry brushes, door mats
and even kettle descalers. Something is
sure to catch your eye.
17 Rugby Street
WC1N 3QT
Tel 0207 430 2526
www.benpentreath.com

AWAY *by* ELIZABETH ANNA HART

AWAY *by* ELIZABETH ANNA HART

AWAY *by* ELIZABETH ANNA HART

AWAY *by* ELIZABETH ANNA HART

AWAY *by* ELIZABETH ANNA HART

2*

MAGGIE OWE

3*

3*

2✴ PERSEPHONE BOOKS

This lovely ramshackle bookshop is dedicated to its own imprint of neglected fiction and non-fiction 'by women, for women and about women'. Delightfully informal, there's a rickety wooden table piled high with books (all in the publisher's distinctive pale grey covers), a jug of flowers and armchairs to settle back and read in. Not slick or styled in any way, the whole place has a charming, unique feel, and the owner's passion for literature shines through.
59 Lamb's Conduit Street
WC1N 3NB
Tel 0207 242 9292
www.persephonebooks.co.uk

3✴ MAGGIE OWEN

Surely one of the prettiest shop fronts in London, this jewellery shop is in a converted dairy, with the original frontage still intact. The pre-war building was London's first dairy, and its heritage is plain to see in the lovely old navy and white shop front tiling and lettering. The dairy itself was a going concern until 1982. These days, the business is a well-chosen mix of contemporary jewellery and accessories, with a few quirky items like Pakistani metal toys and patchwork fabric teddies thrown into the mix. Cast your eye across the street and there's yet more history—writers Ted Hughes and Sylvia Plath spent their wedding night at number 18.
13 Rugby Street
WC1N 3QT
0207 404 7070
www.maggieowenlondon.com

4✻ THE SCHOOL OF LIFE

This unique business could, potentially, change your life. Labelling itself 'an apothecary of ideas and mental wellness' and a 'chemist for the mind', it's both a shop and school in one. Where else can you buy books like *The Mindfulness Manifesto* or *How To Be An Agnostic* and sign up for classes on 'how to have better conversations', 'how to spend time alone' and 'how to balance work with life'? It's a pretty special place. The shop itself is a chic space of dark grey walls painted with the School's manifesto in bold lettering, wooden floors and unexpected touches like a leopard-print couch and silver birch tree-trunks like sculptures growing up from the floor. Even if you leave with just a greetings card, you will feel better for having visited.

70 Marchmont Street
WC1N 1AB
0207 833 1010
www.theschooloflife.com

CLASSES SERMONS WEEKENDS

Take one of our regular evening classes and gain valuable insights into life's big issues.

Bin the Sunday papers and join the congregation at our maverick secular sermons.

Experience intellectual and social adventure on one of our weekends.

235

53

Folk

5✴ FOLK CLOTHING

With two shops on the street, one
menswear, one womenswear, this
mini fashion empire is well worth a visit.
The clothes in both outlets are a mix of
own label and contemporary designers.
Nothing too showy, but all of it confidently
cool. The shops themselves are pared
back and warehouse-like, with strip
lighting hanging from coloured rope and
rough concrete flooring. Look out for the
sculpted marble heads in the menswear
branch by British artist Paul Vanstone.
49 and 53 Lamb's Conduit Street
WC1N 3NB
Women's: Tel 0208 616 4191
Men's: Tel 0207 404 6458
www.folkclothing.com

237

6*

6*

6* OLIVER SPENCER

This lovely, low-key menswear store (with a shoe shop further down the road) prides itself on its British heritage. Most of the clothes are designed and manufactured in the UK, with ninety per cent of them produced under the shop's own label. The style is traditional menswear with a casual, easy-to-wear feel. You won't find anything showy or covered in designer labels here. With its tiled fireplace, old wooden fittings and dark grey walls, the space feels more like a private home than a shop. Look out for the vintage health and hygiene posters on the wall, including one illustrating exercises for men that can be done while still enjoying a cigarette. Those were the days.
62 Lamb's Conduit Street
WC1N 3LW
Tel 0207 269 6444
www.oliverspencer.co.uk

7*

7* CUBE POP-UP SHOP

There's no knowing what this shop will hold next. Thanks to the fashion PR company in the offices behind, it works as a showcase for various clients—a nautical installation of Henri Lloyd sailing gear one week, maybe work by cool young British designer Sophie Hulme the next. Pop by and take a chance.
47 Lamb's Conduit Street
WC1N 3NG
Tel 0207 242 5483
www.cubecompany.com

rhonda drakeford

If you're a fan of unusual, one-off pieces that can't be found elsewhere, then Darkroom is the shop for you. The hand-picked selection of accessories for men, women and the home shines with a love of design and craftsmanship. Owners Rhonda Drakeford and Lulu Roper-Caldbeck are passionate about fusing art and design, so expect to see their own-label collections, one inspired by the 1920s Dutch De Stijl art movement, alongside indigenous African art, textiles and jewellery, and other carefully sourced pieces. Even the shop interior is a design statement, with its boldly geometric black-and-white flooring and black walls. A must-visit.

Darkroom
52 Lamb's Conduit Street WC1N 3LL ❀ 0207 831 7244 ❀ *www.darkroomlondon.com*

'Lounge Bohemia is a brilliant little basement bar serving an unusual array of cocktails'

How would you define London style?
A mix of old and new from here and there.

Where do you go in London to be inspired?
Anywhere with oddities and strange sights, from Ridley Road food market in Dalston to The British Museum (www.britishmuseum.org).

Your favourite local places?
For the best coffee, the Espresso Room on Great Ormond Street (www.theespressoroom.com). For the best fish and chips in London, and brilliant 1960s decor, Fryers Delight (19 Theobald's Road, WC1X 8SL. Tel 0207 405 4114). And for a brilliant array of fruit, veg and provisions, The People's Supermarket on Lamb's Conduit Street (www.thepeoplessupermarket.org).

Describe your perfect out-and-about weekend?
Brunch with friends, a rummage at the Hammersmith Vintage Fair (www.pa-antiques.co.uk), an old film at the British

Film Institute (www.bfi.org.uk) and a hearty, meaty dinner at the **Fox & Anchor** pub near Smithfield (see page 88).

What's in your secret shopping address book?

I buy trimmings and vintage ribbon at **VV Rouleaux** (see page 217) and old-fashioned and beautiful umbrellas at James Smith & Sons (www.james-smith.co.uk).

Where's the best place for a weekend supper?

A Little Of What You Fancy in Dalston (www.alittleofwhatyoufancy.info). When you get past its unassuming exterior—it's easy to miss among a row of dilapidated shops—it's a friendly, informal (and very trendy) little restaurant serving delicious and unpretentious food.

Best place for a drink?

Lounge Bohemia in Shoreditch (www.loungebohemia.com). Again, one that's easily missed—its unmarked door is sandwiched between a fast food takeaway and a t-shirt wholesalers. It's a brilliant little basement bar serving an unusual array of cocktails from menus housed in old books. The service can be slow but the lovely vintage furnishings are a wonderful distraction. Best to book ahead as there's no standing allowed.

Your favourite breakfast spot?

The Wolseley on Piccadilly (www.thewolseley.com). This grand establishment is housed in an old opulently decorated car showroom and it does grand in a non-chintzy way. The breakfasts and afternoon teas make for such a nice treat, without breaking the bank. And St Ali in Clerkenwell (www.stali.co.uk). It's run by Australians who know how to do a good brekkie.

Favourite cultural London sights?

Pearly Kings and Queens in east London. You can seek them out at local fêtes and street parties but catching sight of them by chance, like I once did (a Pearly King and Queen drove past in an old Ford Fiesta on Bethnal Green Road) is so brilliantly strange, it literally makes your day. And I love **Brixton Market** (see page 284) for the plethora of Caribbean food outlets. It's multicultural London at its noisy best.

Top three things that every visitor to London should do?

Go to the Paramount Bar (www.paramount.uk.net) on the top floor of Centre Point for a glamorous way to get one of the best bird's eye views of London. Walk around the ancient parts of the City of London at the weekend, especially Postman's Park near St Paul's Cathedral; there's a fascinating wall of Art Nouveau glazed plaques remembering acts of selflessness and bravery by ordinary people, mostly during the late 1890s. And visit Darkroom, of course!

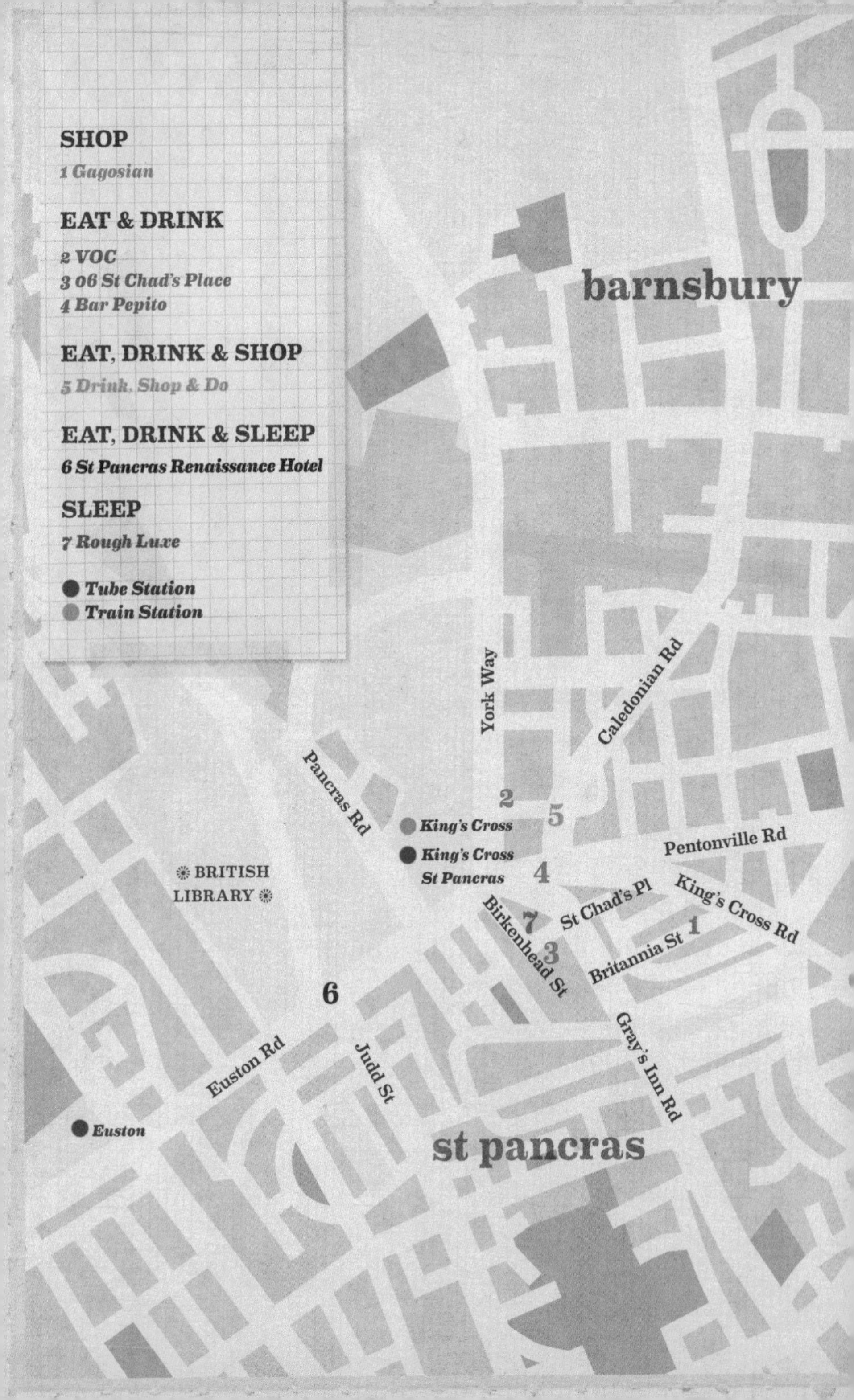

SHOP

1 Gagosian

EAT & DRINK

2 VOC
3 06 St Chad's Place
4 Bar Pepito

EAT, DRINK & SHOP

5 Drink, Shop & Do

EAT, DRINK & SLEEP

6 St Pancras Renaissance Hotel

SLEEP

7 Rough Luxe

● *Tube Station*
● *Train Station*

barnsbury

York Way

Caledonian Rd

Pancras Rd

● King's Cross

● King's Cross
St Pancras

2
5

Pentonville Rd

4

❀ BRITISH
LIBRARY ❀

7 St Chad's Pl

Birkenhead St

King's Cross Rd

3 Britannia St 1

6

Gray's Inn Rd

Euston Rd

Judd St

● Euston

st pancras

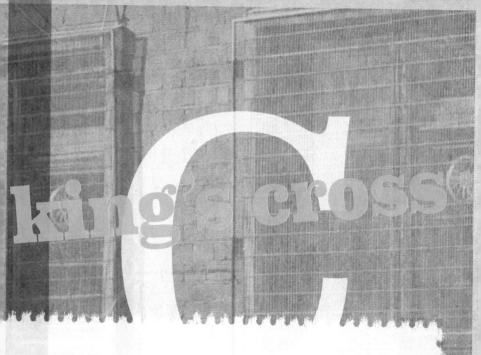

king's cross

One of London's least attractive areas is smartening itself up. The tangle of busy roads around King's Cross train station has never been a must-visit spot, but thanks to a few gems, that's changing. Grandest of all the revamps is the stunning restoration of the St Pancras Renaissance Hotel, a Victorian Gothic masterpiece. Other developments, such as the state-of-the-art **Guardian** newspaper offices, and the transfer of leading London art school St Martins to the area, add to the interest. Granted, you do have to search out the gems, but if all you do is gaze in awe at the architectural beauty of St Pancras and then have a glass of champagne in the bar, your visit will be worthwhile.

GAGOSIAN GALLERY

1 ✳ GAGOSIAN

Add this to your cultural must-visit list. The gallery, part of US dealer Larry Gagosian's mega art empire, hosts some of the most interesting contemporary art shows in town. And not just twenty-first-century working artists—a 2010 Picasso exhibition would have had queues around the block in many cities. Here, only in-the-know Londoners trekked to King's Cross to appreciate it, and like all their other shows, entrance was free. Nondescript from the outside, the gallery opens up into two vast show spaces. Ok, so the artwork may be beyond most people's shopping budget, but the book shop has some more affordable buys. It may be down a scruffy side street and opposite a distinctly unglamorous car park, but some of London's most exciting art world events happen here.

6–24 Britannia Street
WC1X 9JD
Tel 0207 841 9960
www.gagosian.com

2 ✳ VOC

Take a step back to a seventeeth-century drinking den at this tiny, cave-like bar. Modelled on an olde worlde punch house, it's named after the Dutch East India Company (Vereenigde Oost-Indische Compagnie), and is filled with the memorabilia of maritime travels. But the real stars are the drinks themselves. Set among the huge church candles that flicker in this sailors' den, you'll see oak barrels containing all sorts of concoctions. Rums are blended with spices like bergamot and fresh tobacco leaf, a warm gin punch is seasoned with fresh horseradish, pressed apple and vanilla sugar. The tastes are dangerously smooth and quaffable. Tuck yourself into a shadowy corner and go exploring.

2 Varnishers Yard
Regents Quarter
N1 9AW
0207 713 8229
www.voc-london.com

3✳06 ST CHAD'S PLACE

If you didn't know that this stylish bar and restaurant was at the end of this scruffy cobbled side street, chances are you'd walk straight past. It may look unpromising, but do venture beyond the overflowing rubbish bins. The restored brick Victorian warehouse was once a mechanics workshop, long since abandoned, but is now a handsome space, with oversized wooden doors and a large skylight above the tables and Eames-style chairs. A wall-sized blown-up photograph of a train gives a nod to the area's railway heritage. If you can forgive the shabby exterior, it's a very nice place for an evening out.

6 St Chad's Place
WC1X 9HH
Tel 0207 278 3355
www.6stchadsplace.com

4✳BAR PEPITO

Blink and you'll miss this tiny 'bodega' sherry bar. It's a tiny piece of Spain, in the middle of grimy London. With its beautifully patterned, tiled floor and tables fashioned from sherry casks, the bar is the younger sibling of the bigger Camino tapas bar across the courtyard, and it's definitely the more appealing of the two. Choose from the fifteen sherries on offer, order a plate of olives, almonds and hand-carved *jamon*, and transport yourself to Andalucia.

3 Varnishers Yard
N1 9DF
0207 841 7331

5✳ DRINK, SHOP & DO

This Victorian bathhouse has been
transformed into a vintage and craft shop,
with café, and is so unlike anything else
in the area that it has to be visited to
be believed. Quite what the customers
of the adult book shop next door make
of the embroidery patterns and jars of
old-fashioned sweets, it's hard to guess.
The whole place has a jaunty, sunny feel,
from the orange-and-white striped ceiling
to the cheery old fashioned tunes being
played as background music. Come in
here simply to shop—everything you can
see, including the vintage furniture, is for
sale—or sign up for a 'do' craft session,
like a pin-up hair and makeup class.
The café, serving lunch, afternoon tea
and cocktails, is at the back, where the
space unexpectedly opens up under a
huge skylight which floods the space
with light. Hard to think of a nicer spot
for Sunday Scrabble—or one where the
competitor with the highest word score
gets a free cocktail. A little bit of charm
amidst the King's Cross grunge.

9 Caledonian Road
N1 9DX
Tel 0203 343 9138
www.drinkshopdo.com

7✳ROUGH LUXE

Of all the hotels you'd expect to find in this area (many insalubrious and 'pay by the hour'), a quirky design gem is not among them. Describing itself as 'half rough, half luxury', this ten-room establishment is the unique vision of designer Rabih Hage, who has transformed the Grade II listed terrace into a shabby chic wonderland. The 'rough' element comes from walls stripped back to reveal the original plasterwork and fragments of wallpaper, and wooden floors left bare and unvarnished. For the 'luxe', striking artwork from the artists-in-residence, chandeliers, luxurious bed linen and handmade toiletries. Some rooms are tiny, but the design is so impressive that they work. And where else in the area can you breakfast in the garden, on toast and honey from the bees that live on the roof?

1 Birkenhead Street
WC1H 8BA
Tel 0207 837 5338
www.roughluxe.co.uk

255

harry handelsman

A whole book could be devoted to the restoration of the Victorian Gothic building that was originally The Midland Grand Hotel. Opened in 1873 by Queen Victoria, the building had stood derelict for years before being reborn in 2011 as the St Pancras Renaissance Hotel. It is, quite simply, one of London's architectural masterpieces. Splash out and book a room, or just visit the beautiful Gilbert Scott bar for a glass of champagne (less packed and much prettier than the always-busy Booking Office bar). One of the driving forces behind the rescue of the St Pancras is property developer Harry Handelsman, for whom the building is an absolute passion. His Manhattan Loft Corporation has created luxe apartments alongside the hotel, for a lucky few who get to wake up in the midst of all the architectural splendour. There isn't a piece of rare, original wallpaper in the place that Harry doesn't know and love. London owes him a big thank you.

St Pancras Renaissance Hotel
Euston Road NW1 2AR ❋ 0207 841 3540 ❋ www.stpancrasrenaissance.co.uk

> 'We are so spoilt in London as there are so many parks and open spaces'

How would you define London style?
Laidback, cool and creative.

Where do you go in London to be inspired?
London has so many places you can go to be inspired. I love the Tate Modern (www.tate.org.uk) because they always have such wonderfully thoughtful exhibitions. I also love opera, and to be able to enjoy it in such beautiful surroundings as The Royal Opera House (www.roh.org.uk) is a real treat.

Your favourite local places?
I still love the Groucho Club (www.thegrouchoclub.com). It is so effortlessly cool, and it's close to my office so I go there a lot.

Describe your perfect out-and-about weekend?
My perfect weekend would involve cycling round Hyde Park on Boris Bikes with my daughter, having a coffee by the Serpentine and taking in an exhibition at the Royal Academy (www.royalacademy.org.uk). We are so spoilt in London as there are

257

so many parks and open spaces, so many wonderful museums and such beautiful architecture.

What's in your secret shopping address book?

Spencer Hart on Savile Row are the best tailors in London in my opinion (www.spencerhart.com). For grooming, I go to Carmelo Guastella, who owns the fantastic Melogy Men's Grooming Ltd (www.melogy.com). He is utterly charming and men come from all over London get their hair cut by him. I recently gave my daughter a bag from Bottega Veneta (www.bottegaveneta. com)—she was thrilled! And I also think Anya Hindmarch (www. anyahindmarch.com) makes the most beautiful bags.

Where's the best place for a weekend supper?

I love Pizza East Portobello on Portbello Road (www.pizzaeastportobello.com). It is tiny, but with delicious pizzas, a great atmosphere and friendly service.

Best place for a drink?

The Cigar Bar at Claridges (www. claridges.co.uk), it is so elegant and refined.

Your favourite breakfast sptot?

The Booking Office at the St Pancras Renaissance Hotel—I am there for breakfast at least three times a week so it's lucky I like it. It is the old Victorian ticket booking office and you can still see all the original features like the ticket booth windows. I also love to be able to look out of the window onto the St Pancras train station platform and see the Eurostar coming and going. The food is also delicious with fantastic service; it's a great way to start the day.

Where do you go in London to relax?

Hyde Park, it is so beautiful.

Favourite cultural London sights?

I like to be challenged by art so one of my favourite galleries is White Cube in Hoxton Square (www.whitecube.com). A visit there is always enlightening. They show very high quality work and there are always interesting people popping in and out. I also like the Albert Memorial in Hyde Park. It was designed by Sir George Gilbert Scott who was also the architect of the St Pancras Renaissance Hotel. I have a new-found respect for him now.

Top three things that every visitor to London should do?

Ride a Boris Bike in Hyde Park— I think these rent-by-the-hour bikes will become as much a part of London imagery as red buses and black taxis. It's a really great scheme, so easy to use and a great way to see London. Go to The Proms at the Royal Albert Hall (www.royalalberthall.com), it is such an English tradition. Obviously the last night is the most famous, but you are guaranteed a wonderful evening on any Prom night. I went three times last year. Finally, walk around. There is so much to see and do in London. It is such a wonderful, vibrant city that even just by strolling around you can feel uplifted and inspired. I have lived here for twenty years and still I can walk around and see things that I have never noticed before. It is a revelation.

259

SHOP
1 *Lina Stores*
2 *Pertwee Anderson & Gold*

EAT & DRINK
3 *Randall & Aubin*
4 *Experimental Cocktail Club*
5 *Lantana*
6 *Riding House Café*
7 *Bistro du Vin*
8 *Tapped and Packed*
9 *Polpo*

EAT, DRINK & SLEEP
10 *Charlotte Street Hotel*
11 *Dean Street Townhouse*

● *Tube Station*

noho

● *Goodge Street*   Store St

❊ THE BRITISH
MUSEUM ❊

Tottenham Court Rd

Goodge St   5   Charlotte St

6   10

Mortimer St   Great Titchfield St   Rathbone Pl

8

● *Tottenham Court Road*

Oxford St

● *Oxford Circus*

Berwick St   Dean St   7

Great Marlborough St   Poland St   11   2   Charing Cross Rd

Bateman St

soho

Regent St   Beak St   9

Brewer St   1   3   Shaftesbury Ave   Gerrard St   4

● *Leicester Square*

● *Piccadilly Circus*

soho & noho

Chances are you'll be heading to Oxford Street to do some shopping at some point during your stay. Chances are you'll want to get the hell out of there as soon as possible. The big name stores are great, the crowds are not. Head down one of the many side streets north or south, and you'll find yourself in the small streets of Soho and Noho (as the area to the north has been christened). Yes, Soho was once known for its sleaze and sex shops, but these days it's home to some of London's best bars and restaurants. Many are Michelin-starred establishments, but there has been an explosion of fantastic, great-value cafés and small restaurants, and you'd be mad to miss them. You'll need a drink after those Oxford Street hordes.

1✱LINA STORES

This charming family-run Italian delicatessen is a Soho institution. It was given a makeover last year, but its distinctive green and white tiling and thick marble countertop remain unchanged. Famous for its homemade pasta, it also sells pretty much any Italian foodstuff you can think of, from polenta, rice and biscotti, to salamis, cheeses and home-made pesto. As for olive oil, take your pick from over fifteen varieties. Grab a coffee from the counter at the back, browse the shelves and buy yourself something delicious to take home.

18 Brewer Street
W1F 0SH
Tel 0207 437 6482
www.linastores.co.uk

263

10*

10*

10*

10*

2✳ PERTWEE ANDERSON & GOLD

In the market for some artwork? This small gallery, co-owned by actor Sean Pertwee, is the perfect place to start. In contrast to the usual architectural white cube style of exhibition spaces, this has been reconstructed to resemble a Georgian house. With dark wood floors and intricate white cornicing, it eschews the sterile art house look for the chic and elegant feel of a gentleman's club. Big spenders get to enter through a jungle-like garden at the back of the house—who knew there were palm trees in Soho?—and peruse their purchases in a cosy faux Georgian boudoir, complete with red velvet sofas and dark parquetry floor. The rest of us might not be so lucky, but it's definitely worth popping in, even if it is through the front door.

15 Bateman Street
W1D 3AQ
Tel 0207 734 9283
www.pertweeandersongold.com

10✳ CHARLOTTE STREET HOTEL

Another of Kit Kemp's London hotels (see page 72), the fifty-two-room Charlotte Street Hotel is a brilliantly central city base to stay, but also the perfect spot for an early evening drink. Do as the local workers do; if the weather's nice, grab a table beneath the stripy awnings on the pavement-side terrace (next to the outsize tubs of olive trees) and watch the street life go by. Cosier evenings in the bar are just as fun, with its warm tones of pink and purple velvets, and striped and kilim-patterned upholstery. The hotel also has a small private screening room, with a regular Sunday film club of dinner and a movie. A lovely way to round off the weekend.

15–17 Charlotte Street
W1T 1RJ
Tel 0207 806 2000
www.firmdale.com

3 ✳ RANDALL & AUBIN

The heritage of this restaurant is clear
from its lovely gold-lettered shop front.
It was opened in 1911 as a butcher's,
by Morin Randall and Cavenur Aubin
whose names are resplendent above the
door. A restaurant since 1996, it retains
all the charm and history of the original
establishment, but these days it does a
brisk trade in champagne and oysters
rather than pork chops. And I doubt
Messrs Randall and Aubin would have
thought much of the chandeliers and
glitter ball. Most nights, there's a queue
of Soho's bright young things sipping
drinks as they wait for a seat at one of
the marble-top benches. But the seafood
and rotisserie menu is worth the wait.
A little bit of Victoriana brought lovingly
up to date.
16 Brewer Street
W1F 0SQ
Tel 0207 287 4447
www.randallandaubin.com

4✳

4 ✳ EXPERIMENTAL
COCKTAIL CLUB

It's easy to walk straight past this
speakeasy-style bar in Chinatown. The
shabby doorway amid the Peking duck
restaurants and Chinese supermarkets of
Gerrard Street gives nothing away. Nor do
the scruffily carpeted stairs that you have
to climb once you're inside. But persevere,
because this tiny two-storey spot serves
some of London's best cocktails, in a cool,
shabby chic interior. Settle yourself at one
of the small, mirrored tables and toast
the night with the likes of a Winnie The
Pooh (rum, campari and a few extras) or
a No Name Dropping (including sherry
and ginseng liqueur). One tip: try to make
a booking, it will make navigating the
attitude of the doorman infinitely easier.
13a Gerrard Street
W1D 5PS
Tel 07825 215 877
www.chinatownecc.com

267

5*

5

6*

6

5✳ LANTANA

Describing itself as a 'little bit of Australia' in the heart of London, this tiny café is pretty much always packed. Breakfast is especially busy—no surprise, with a menu of toasted banana bread with blossom honey and cinnamon labna, and grilled haloumi with roast cherry tomatoes, rocket and red onion salad, poached egg and pesto on toasted sourdough. Londoners aren't used to such an Antipodean blend of flavours, and they are lapping it up. Decor-wise, things are kept simple, with the space dominated by a black and white mural on the back wall, by Melbourne artist Kat Macleod. Depicting the invasive weed lantana, after which the café is named, the artwork also features other Aussie flora and fauna, to remind any visiting Australians of home.
13 Charlotte Place
W1T 1SN
Tel 0207 637 3347
www.lantanacafe.co.uk

6✳ RIDING HOUSE CAFÉ

Squirrels on the walls and some of the friendliest staff in London—what's not to love about this place? With the feel of a New York brasserie, but with delightfully quirky touches (like those squirrel wall lights), this bar and restaurant has drawn crowds from day one. Book one of the sexy booths in the main restaurant, or for a more casual meal, perch up at the bar or at the huge communal table with its nailed down cinema seats as chairs. Food ranges from 'small plates' to share (beetroot carpaccio with sheep's ricotta, cured sea trout with jalapeno and crème fraiche) through to the ever-popular Titchfield Burger with foie gras. The private dining room, The Stables, describes itself as 'an equestrian lodge'. The mind boggles.
43–51 Great Titchfield Street
W1W 7PQ
0207 927 0840
www.ridinghousecafe.co.uk

7✳ BISTRO DU VIN

Better known for its chain of stylishly affordable hotels (none in London, unfortunately), the Hotel du Vin group now has two stand-alone Bistro du Vins, one in Clerkenwell and one in Soho. Both are worth a pop-in, but Soho has the edge for being one of the few places in this always-busy neighbourhood where you know you can get a drink and a seat (the two rarely go together around here, unless you're dining). Sit up at the long brasserie-style bar, grab yourself a booth or head for the cosy lounge at the back with its multicoloured bookshelves and comfy armchairs. Don't leave without sampling the delights of the La Cave à Fromage, a walk-in cheese room that takes some beating, accompanied by a glass of something from the master sommelier's impressive 200+ wine list.

36 Dean Street
W1D 4PS
Tel 0207 432 4800
www.bistroduvinandbar.com

8✳ TAPPED AND PACKED

Coffee is a very serious business at this small side-street café. Generally regarded as one of London's best barista spots, its motto is 'making the ordinary, extraordinary'. Which means high quality fixtures and fittings— lovely solid wooden tables and benches, nicely weighty cups and quirky vintage spoons—as well as coffee beans from artisan roasteries and a small menu of simple but delicious snacks. Local workers claim the breakfast toast is the tastiest and best-value in all London. Well worth a detour if you're shopping on Oxford Street and want to rest your weary legs.

26 Rathbone Place
W1T 1JD
www.tappedandpacked.co.uk

8*

'Generally regarded as one of London's best barista spots, its motto is "making the ordinary, extraordinary"'

271

11✳ DEAN STREET TOWNHOUSE

Overnight locations don't come more in-the-thick-of-it than smack bang in the centre of Soho. This thirty-nine-bedroom boutique hotel, spread over two Georgian townhouses, is in the heart of the action, but the hotel itself is so seductive that you might be tempted to stay put. Rooms range from Tiny (fifteen square metres) up to Bigger, but whatever the dimensions, they're all slick, beautifully designed and luxurious. Broom Cupboard may be little more than a crash-pad, but it's a gorgeous one, with a small en suite that outdoes what many larger hotel rooms can offer. If you can, treat yourself to a Bigger, and enjoy a four-poster bed with a deep roll-top bath at the end of it. Very sexy. Design throughout the hotel is cosy glam, with lots of velvet upholstery, dark wood, chandeliers and flickering candles. More like a country house than a heart-of-the-city abode. The hotel's bar and restaurant is permanently crammed with Londoners. No wonder. With discerning regulars like Nigella Lawson (she has a favourite breakfast table), artwork from the likes of Tracy Emin and Peter Blake on the walls and a menu that offers traditional British dishes with a twist, it's one of the city's most grown-up and gorgeous spots.

69–71 Dean Street
W1D 3SE
Tel 0207 434 1775
www.deanstreettownhouse.com

russell norman

To open one tiny no-bookings restaurant in Soho, and have it packed from
day one, is quite an achievement. To add two more Soho sites in swift
succession, plus two in Covent Garden, makes you a legend in restaurant
circles. Russell Norman's empire now includes Polpo (the original), Polpetto,
Da Polpo and Spuntino. Inspired by the scruffy bars of downtown New York,
and the 'bacari' bars of Venice that serve 'cicheti' bar snacks, the restaurants
share a casual, cool scruffiness and an absolute dedication to delicious food.
And Russell's not done yet. He's added Mishkin's to the mix, a place he calls
'a sort of sexy, fun version of a Jewish deli'. The man's unstoppable.

❧ **Polpo—41 Beak Street W1F 9SB ❧ 0207 734 4479 ❧ www.polpo.co.uk**
❧ **Polpetto—2nd floor, French House 49 Dean Street W1D 5BG ❧ 0207 734 1969**
   www.polpetto.co.uk
❧ **Da Polpo—6 Maiden Lane WC2E 7NW ❧ 0207 836 8448 ❧ www.dapolpo.co.uk**
❧ **Spuntino—61 Rupert Street W1D 7PW ❧ www.spuntino.co.uk**
❧ **Mishkin's—25 Catherine Street WC2B 5JS ❧ 0207 240 2078 ❧ www.mishkins.co.uk**

'I have a perverse admiration for Centre Point. It's like an immense cheese grater'

How would you define London style?

London has a split personality. It's conservative and traditional on one hand, but edgy and progressive on the other. Mayfair v. Shoreditch, for example. London style is massively eclectic. We Londoners don't have the swagger and confidence of, say, New Yorkers, and consequently the city lacks the intense energy of the Big Apple. But London style is more sophisticated and understated.

Where do you go in London to be inspired?

Standing in the middle of Waterloo bridge is pretty inspiring, but so is having a cup of tea outside Maison Bertaux in Soho (www.maisonbertaux.com) and watching the world go by. I always get a thrill at the British Library (www.bl.uk), particularly from the huge Eduardo Paolozzi sculpture of Newton, After William Blake in the Library piazza. I also have a perverse admiration for Centre Point (www.centrepointlondon.com), architect Richard Seifert's glorious 1960s concrete monolith. It's like an immense cheese grater.

Your favourite local places?

Parliament Hill, Regent's Park Zoo (www.zsl.org), Blackheath, the mixed bathing pond on Hampstead Heath, the Royal Observatory in Greenwich (www.nmm.ac.uk) and Berwick Street Market. They're nearly all places that make me feel like I'm not in London. My working week is intensely urban and full of people, so those local places I enjoy tend to offer the opposite. Berwick Street is the odd one out, but I've listed it because it's so much a part of my world.

What's in your secret shopping address book?

I Camisa (www.camisa.co.uk), a traditional Italian deli in Soho, You Don't Bring Me Flowers (www.youdon'tbringmeflowers.co.uk), an evocative and dainty tea shop/florist in Hither Green and Play Lounge (www.playlounge.co.uk), a great cartoon and toy shop on Beak Street—they have original Totoro merchandise. There are other shops I couldn't do without, but they're hardly secret, like Liberty's menswear department (www.liberty.co.uk), which always carries an artfully curated collection of classics and slightly cutting edge pieces. I rarely get away without making a purchase.

Where's the best place for a weekend supper?

At home with my wife and children. On rare date nights out, we like to start with a spritz at Polpo's Campari bar and then have supper at one of my places—Polpetto is the most romantic—or somewhere informal where the food is great. We also like Roka (www.rokarestaurant.com) in Fitzrovia and Koya (www.koya.co.uk) in Soho.

Best place for a drink?

The Dog & Duck (18 Bateman Street, W1D 3AJ. Tel 0207 494 0697) is the best pub in Soho. Everyone knows that. It pulls a great pint of Timothy Taylor's Landlord. The best pub in London, however, is the Jerusalem Tavern in Clerkenwell (www.stpetersbrewery.co.uk).

Your favourite breakfast spot?

Breakfast is for wimps. I'll have an espresso from **Lina Stores** (see page 262). If I have a very early start and find hunger pangs interfering with my concentration, I might treat myself to a bacon sarnie on white bread from Bar Bruno (101 Wardour Street, W1F OUG. Tel 0207 734 3750), one of the last remaining greasy spoons in Soho.

Where do you go in London to relax?

I can never relax. I go to the Third Space gymnasium (www.thirdspace.com) on Sherwood Street, instead.

Favourite London cultural sights?

The National Theatre (www.nationaltheatre.org.uk) on the South Bank is my favourite cultural destination. The level and quality of theatre there is always superb. And I'm one of the only people I know who loves the building, too. It's a concrete masterpiece that looks more amazing with every passing year.

Top 3 things that every visitor to London should do?

Take the Thames Clipper from Westminster to Greenwich (www.thamesclippers.com), London looks totally different from the water. Be photographed on the Abbey Road zebra crossing (www.abbeyroad.com)—it's surprisingly impressive to stand there and be transported back to the iconic Beatles' album cover—and go to Tate Modern (www.tate.org.uk), it really is the most jaw-droppingly brilliant gallery, and it's free.

off the map

X

Too good to leave out just because they don't fit into any of the book's chapters, these are a few standout favourites that deserve a mention. Of course, London is filled with many more must-see spots, and the beauty of the city is that there's always somewhere new to stumble across. These are just a few that are worth seeking out if you're in the area—no doubt you'll discover some more favourites of your own.

1❋ PETERSHAM NURSERIES

Leave the city behind and head to green
and pleasant Richmond, for one of the
most picturesque eating and shopping
spots in London. Set in the actual working
Victorian nurseries of Petersham House,
the Michelin-starred restaurant is run
by Australian head chef Skye Gyngell.
(It must be the first Michelin star awarded
to an eatery with garden dirt flooring.)
Flavours are fresh and seasonal, with a
short menu of simple dishes, all featuring
herbs, salads and fruit from the Estate's
gardens. But it's the location that delights,
as much as what is on the plate. In a word,
magical. From the greenhouse setting of
the restaurant itself, to the adjacent shop
offering plants and small bits and pieces of
homeware, not to mention the surrounding
lush Thames-side water meadows, this
really is an idyllic spot. Hard to believe that
central London is just a few miles away.
Church Lane, off Petersham Road
Petersham, near Richmond
Surrey TW10 7AG
Tel 0208 940 5230
www.petershamnurseries.com

281

2✳ DOVER STREET MARKET

Not so much a shop as a collective of fashion installations under one roof, Mayfair's Dover Street Market is a non-negotiable destination for anyone who appreciates stylish shopping. Opened in 2004 by Rei Kawakubo of Comme des Garçons, it stocks the world's most cutting-edge labels, many of them, like Azzedine Alaia, Lanvin and Celine, with their own mini-spaces conceived as one-off experiences by the designers themselves. (The shop closes twice a year for a two-day 'Tachiagari' refit, when the likes of designers Rick Owens, Phoebe Philo and Alber Elbaz personally oversee the new configurations.) Walking in to the ground floor of concrete flooring, fantastical chandeliers and a display cabinet of skulls, it's impossible to imagine what awaits you on all six levels. And when retail fatigue kicks in, head to the delicious Rose Bakery on the fourth floor for a cup of tea and cake. A unique shopping experience.

17–18 Dover Street
W1S 4LT
Tel 0207 518 0680
www.doverstreetmarket.com

3✳ THE CROSS

London's original boho chic bolthole in Holland Park is still going strong. Its stock of women's clothes and accessories, plus the odd bit of vintage furniture, is a kaleidoscope of colours, patterns and textures. If you're a fan of head-to-toe black, this is not the place for you. Think luxe hippy chic—these are clothes to have fun in. Even the shop decor will put you in a good mood, with its strings of bright paper lanterns, fairy lights and quirky decorative details. The building, on the corner of a street of pastel-coloured, stuccoed houses is about as picturesque as it gets.

141 Portland Road
W11 4LR
Tel 0207 727 6760
www.thecrossshop.co.uk

3*

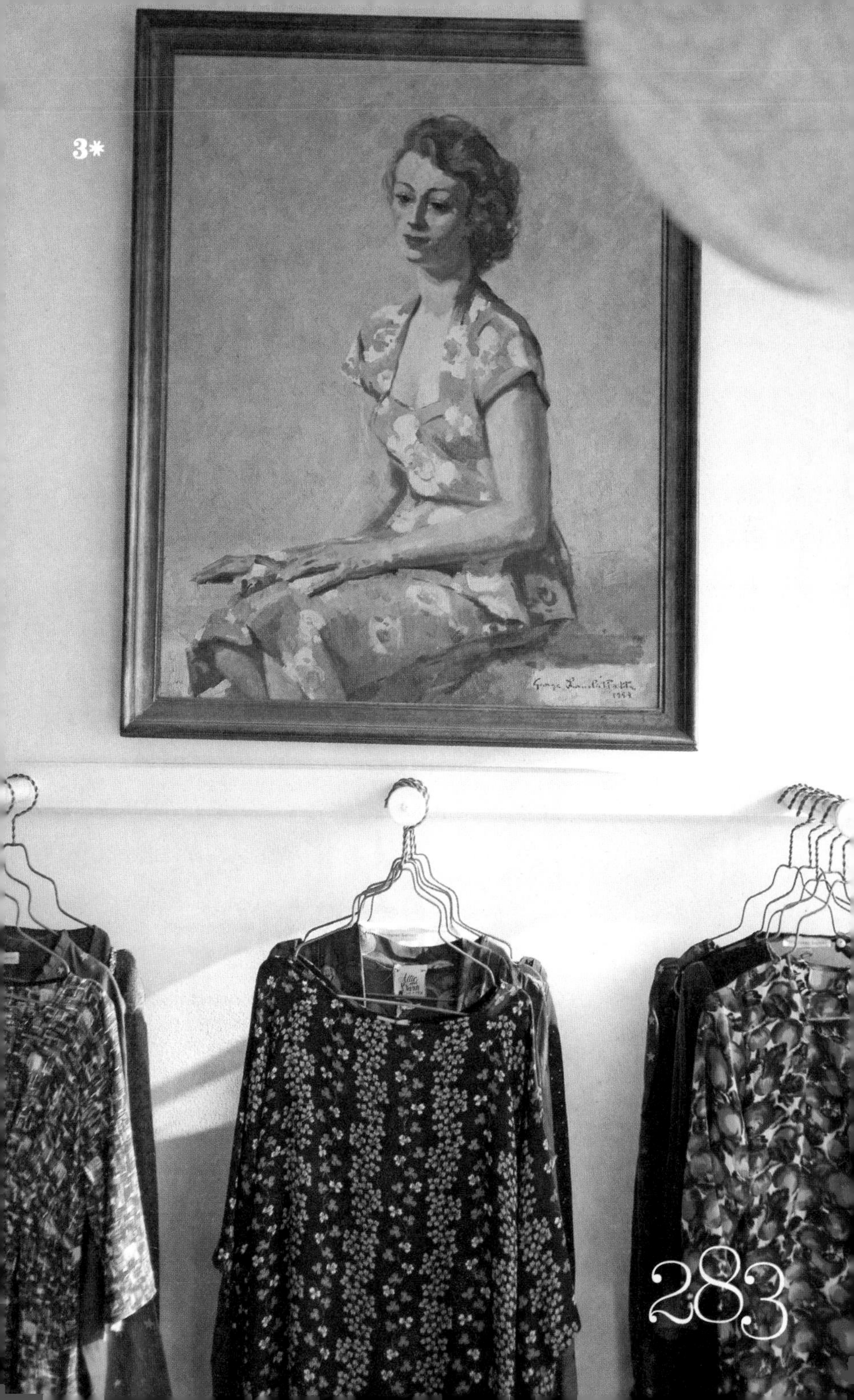

4 ❋ BRIXTON VILLAGE

This book's photographers Jess and
Martin rate this as one of their favourite
haunts in London. And certainly foodies
cannot get enough of the smorgasbord of
restaurants and shops in Brixton Village,
the 1930s market arcade that has been
rescued and revitalised in recent years.
If you want to experience, under one
roof, the tastes of the myriad cultures
that exist in London, this is the place to
come. It may not be as polished as many
of the venues featured in this book but the
market's atmosphere is electric, especially
on Thursday and Friday nights when
it stays open late. There are too many
culinary temptations for just one visit, but
ones to put on your menu include Thai at
family-run KaoSarn, rare breed Yorkshire
pig burgers at Honest Burgers, irresistible
sourdough breads and on-site roasted
coffee at Breads Etcetera, and exotic store
cupboard buys like chilli and mango
ketchup at Brixton Cornercopia.

Granville Arcade
Atlantic Road
SW9 8PS
www.honestburgers.co.uk
www.breadsetceterabakery.com
www.brixtoncornercopia.ning.com

5✳ THE WAPPING PROJECT

The Wapping Project is a cultural and architectural hymn to East London past and present. The converted nineteenth-century hydraulic power station hosts a cutting-edge art gallery and book shop (in the garden's greenhouse), but for the best experience of this Grade II listed industrial gem, head to the restaurant in the main hall nestled among the power station's original machinery. By night, candles are placed on giant chunks of green metal and rusting beams, while exposed brick and huge black pipes create a stunning backdrop. The menu is fresh and seasonal and the wine list extensive. East London at its best.

Wapping Hydraulic Power Station
Wapping Wall
E1W 3SG
Tel 0207 680 2080
www.thewappingproject.com

6✳ GRANGER & CO. WESTBOURNE GROVE

At last, London has its own outpost of Australian restaurateur Bill Granger's café empire. Having moved to the city two years ago, he's finally opened his first place in his favourite neighbourhood of Notting Hill. (He lives just around the corner so you can be sure he'll be keeping a close eye on proceedings.) The bright, light and airy dining room has all the beloved trademarks of Bills Sydney café: easy, breezy food with a decidedly Aussie feel, sleek, clean interior design and a great cup of coffee. It's been a long time coming, but well worth the wait.

175 Westbourne Grove
W11 2SB
Tel 0207 229 9111
www.grangerandco.com

7 ✷ UPSTAIRS AT RULES

The restaurant downstairs is one of the oldest in London, founded in 1798 and famous for its traditional British dishes like game and oysters. But it's the cocktail bar, Upstairs at Rules, that is the insider's secret—there's minimal signage. Simply ask the restaurant's doorman, and he will open a discreet side door and usher you up the stairs. At the top, a dark-wood room decorated with hunting scene murals, old-fashioned tassled light fittings and patterned carpets. With its red leather chairs and red velvet booths, it has the feel of a gentleman's club, all very horse and hounds. It's a quiet, undiscovered spot, perfect for avoiding the Covent Garden crowds and enjoying a grown-up cocktail or two.

35 Maiden Lane
Covent Garden
WC2E 7LB
Tel 0207 836 5314

289

barny read

When a blackboard sign outside a shop has an arrow and the handwritten message 'Good Shop', you'd be mad to walk past. Inside the Peanut Vendor's small space in North London's Newington Green, you'll find vintage design heaven, with a range of well-priced mid-century furniture and oddities. Owner Barny Read has a self-confessed obsession with anything old, be it records, clothes or furniture. And, along with co-owner Becky Nolan, he's turned it into his business. You might spot an industrial trolley, a stack of old school chairs or even a stuffed pigeon. This is a beautifully edited selection of quirky and cool buys, not a bit of junk in sight. Barny is passionate about finding great pieces and selling them at affordable prices—many other places would be charging a lot more—and a love of the merchandise shines through.

The Peanut Vendor
133 Newington Green Road N1 4RA ❀ 0207 226 5727 ❀ www.thepeanutvendor.co.uk

> *'I love all the old buildings, there are hidden gems all over the city'*

How would you define London style?
I think a lot of people my age like to buy into heritage brands. I guess it's the safety of knowing something is done well. Having said that, a lot of younger Londoners make their look work by styling charity shop and vintage finds well.

Where do you go in London to be inspired?
Everywhere I've lived in London I'd go for a wander and be inspired. I love all the old buildings, there are hidden gems all over the city.

Your favourite local places?
Newington Green Fruit And Vegetables (109 Newington Green Rd, N1 4QY. Tel 0207 354 0990) is definitely the best fruit-and-veg shop in London. Belle Epoque (www. belleepoque.co.uk) is an amazing French patisserie on Newington Green—the crumbles are another level, but nothing in there ever disappoints.

291

Describe your perfect out-and-about weekend?

A trip to a farmers' market to pick up some good meats, a bike ride somewhere, preferably near a good coffee, and then a wander round looking in some record shops. In an ideal world, I'd end up at Plastic People, a club in Shoreditch (www.plasticpeople.co.uk) watching Dixon play. Cab home and then breakfast at local café Acoustic (60 Newington Green, N16 9PX. Tel 0207 288 1235).

What's in your secret shopping address book?

Opposite our flat is probably my favourite shop in London. It's called Sargent & Co (www.sargentandco.com) and sells bespoke bikes. It's exactly what a bike shop should be, an organised mess full of beautiful vintage frames. The smell of bike oil hits you the minute you walk through the door and every time I go past I want a new bike. Rob, the owner hand-picks them and fixes them up to order.

Where's the best place for a weekend supper?

Trullo in Islington (www.trullorestaurant.com). It's just round the corner from the shop, off Highbury Corner. Really great Italian food and beautifully done out, a real treat.

Best place for a drink?

The Island Queen in Islington (www.theislandqueenislington.co.uk) is always nice. It's close to the canal so you can cycle along that to get there. It's a little bit tucked away so never too busy. And The Charles Lamb (www.thecharleslambpub.com) round the corner is good for food.

Your favourite breakfast spot?

Acoustic in Newington Green, for three reasons: One. I love the owner. Two. It's about ten metres from the shop and three, the food is always tasty and very reasonably priced.

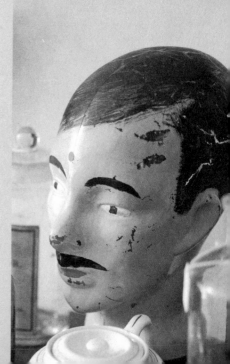

293

about the author

Saska Graville has worked as a writer and editor in women's magazines and newspapers for over twenty years, both in London and Sydney. She was the editor of New Woman magazine, Australia, and the features editor of The Sun-Herald newspaper in Sydney, before moving back to London as deputy editor of bestselling glossy magazine Red. She remains a UK travel correspondent for The Sun-Herald, and loves nothing more than a new hotel to review.

A BIG THANK YOU

This book could not have happened without the help of four people. First, the dynamic duo husband-and-wife photographic team of Jess Reftel Evans and Martin Reftel. Their energy and enthusiasm is infectious. Second, my co-researcher Alison Bakunowich, who paced the streets of London alongside me most weekends and made the whole project infinitely more fun. And lastly, Red magazine's interiors and food director Mary Norden, who helped to brainstorm the book idea in the first place. Thanks also to Red's editor-in-chief Sam Baker and picture director Beverley Croucher for all their help and support, to Marisa Bate for her additional research, and to the team at Murdoch Books—my publisher Tracy Lines, project editor Sophia Oravecz and designer Miriam Steenhauer—who have all been more than a pleasure to work with. And a final thank you to all of the Londoners who I encountered along the way. You're an inspiring lot and we live in a brilliant city. We should all be very proud.

Published in 2012 by Murdoch Books Pty Limited

Murdoch Books Australia
Pier 8/9
Millers Point NSW 2000
Phone: +61 (0) 2 8220 2000
Fax: +61 (0) 2 8220 2558
www.murdochbooks.com.au
info@murdochbooks.com.au
www.murdochbooks.co.uk

Murdoch Books UK Limited
Erico House, 6th Floor
23 Hickson Road
93–99 Upper Richmond Road
Putney, London SW15 2TG
Phone: +44 (0) 20 8785 5995
Fax: +44 (0) 20 8785 5985
info@murdochbooks.co.uk

For Corporate Orders & Custom Publishing contact Noel Hammond,
National Business Development Manager Murdoch Books Australia

Publisher: Tracy Lines
Design concept: Tracy Lines
Designer: Miriam Steenhauer
Cover design: Miriam Steenhauer
Photographers: Jessica Reftel Evans and Martin Reftel
Project editor: Sophia Oravecz
Production: Karen Small
Maps: Netmaps®

National Library of Australia Cataloguing-in-Publication entry
    Graville, Saska.
    London style guide : eat sleep shop / Saska Graville.
    978-1-74266-758-4 (hbk.)
    Restaurants—England—London—Guidebooks.
    Bars (Drinking establishments)—England—London—Guidebooks.
    Shopping—England—London—Guidebooks.
    London (England)—Description and travel—21st century.
    London (England)—Guidebooks.
    914.210486

A catalogue record for this book is available from the British Library.

Printed by 1010 Printing International Limited, China

All details referred to in this book were correct at the time of printing.
Please contact the venues directly as the details are subject to change.